50 Delicious Fruit Dessert Recipes for Home

By: Kelly Johnson

Table of Contents

- Lobster Thermidor
- Beef Wellington
- Chicken Marsala
- Shrimp Scampi
- Filet Mignon
- Duck à l'Orange
- Coq au Vin
- Veal Saltimbocca
- Stuffed Chicken Breast
- Grilled Lamb Chops
- Seafood Paella
- Osso Buco
- Rack of Lamb
- Chateaubriand
- Bouillabaisse
- Seared Scallops
- Eggplant Parmesan
- Chicken Piccata
- Salmon en Croûte
- Pork Tenderloin with Apple Cider Reduction
- Baked Halibut with Herb Butter
- Risotto Milanese
- Beef Stroganoff
- Moroccan Lamb Tagine
- Crab Cakes
- Sole Meunière
- Stuffed Bell Peppers
- Grilled Tuna Steak
- Lemon Herb Roast Chicken
- Shrimp and Grits
- Mushroom Risotto
- Spaghetti Carbonara
- Chicken Alfredo
- Veal Marsala
- Baked Ziti
- Grilled Swordfish

- Duck Breast with Raspberry Sauce
- Stuffed Portobello Mushrooms
- Pan-Seared Sea Bass
- Tortellini Alfredo
- Steak Diane
- Fettuccine Alfredo with Shrimp
- Lamb Shank
- Herb-Crusted Salmon
- Chicken Cordon Bleu
- Grilled Ribeye Steak
- Shrimp Fra Diavolo
- Pork Chops with Sage Butter
- Seafood Risotto
- Spinach and Ricotta Stuffed Shells

Lobster Thermidor

Ingredients:

- 2 whole lobsters (1 1/2 to 2 pounds each)
- 1/4 cup unsalted butter
- 1 small shallot, finely chopped
- 1 clove garlic, minced
- 1/2 cup dry white wine
- 1/2 cup heavy cream
- 1/4 cup grated Parmesan cheese
- 1/4 cup Gruyère cheese, grated
- 2 teaspoons Dijon mustard
- 2 teaspoons lemon juice
- Salt and freshly ground black pepper, to taste
- 1 tablespoon chopped fresh parsley
- 1 tablespoon chopped fresh tarragon
- 1/4 cup breadcrumbs

Instructions:

1. Prepare the Lobsters:
    - Bring a large pot of salted water to a boil.
    - Add the lobsters and cook for 8-10 minutes, until bright red.
    - Remove lobsters and let cool. Once cool, split them in half lengthwise and remove the meat. Set aside the lobster shells for later use.
2. Make the Sauce:
    - In a medium saucepan, melt the butter over medium heat.
    - Add the shallot and garlic, and cook until softened, about 2-3 minutes.
    - Pour in the white wine and let it reduce by half.
    - Add the heavy cream and bring to a simmer.
    - Stir in the Parmesan and Gruyère cheeses until melted and smooth.
    - Mix in the Dijon mustard, lemon juice, salt, and pepper.
    - Add the chopped parsley and tarragon. Remove from heat.
3. Combine Lobster and Sauce:
    - Chop the lobster meat into bite-sized pieces and fold into the sauce.
    - Spoon the mixture back into the reserved lobster shells.
4. Top and Bake:
    - Preheat your oven's broiler.
    - Sprinkle the breadcrumbs over the filled lobster shells.
    - Place the filled shells on a baking sheet and broil for 3-5 minutes, or until the top is golden brown and bubbly.
5. Serve:
    - Remove from the oven and let cool slightly before serving.
    - Garnish with additional parsley if desired.

Enjoy your romantic Lobster Thermidor dinner!

Beef Wellington

Ingredients:

- 2 beef fillet steaks (about 6 oz each)
- Salt and freshly ground black pepper, to taste
- 2 tablespoons olive oil
- 1 tablespoon Dijon mustard
- 1 tablespoon unsalted butter
- 1 shallot, finely chopped
- 2 cloves garlic, minced
- 8 oz cremini mushrooms, finely chopped
- 1 tablespoon fresh thyme leaves
- 1/4 cup dry white wine
- 4 slices prosciutto
- 1 sheet puff pastry, thawed
- 1 egg, beaten
- 1 tablespoon water

Instructions:

1. Prepare the Steaks:
    - Season the beef fillets with salt and pepper.
    - Heat the olive oil in a pan over high heat.
    - Sear the steaks for 1-2 minutes on each side until browned. Remove from pan and let cool.
    - Brush the Dijon mustard over the cooled steaks.
2. Make the Duxelles:
    - In the same pan, melt the butter over medium heat.
    - Add the shallot and garlic, cooking until softened, about 2-3 minutes.
    - Add the chopped mushrooms and thyme, cooking until the mushrooms release their moisture and become dry.
    - Pour in the white wine and cook until evaporated. Season with salt and pepper, and let cool.
3. Assemble the Wellington:
    - Lay a sheet of plastic wrap on a work surface.
    - Arrange the prosciutto slices in a layer, overlapping slightly.
    - Spread half of the mushroom mixture over the prosciutto.
    - Place one steak in the center and wrap the prosciutto around it using the plastic wrap to form a tight bundle. Repeat with the other steak. Refrigerate for 15-20 minutes.
4. Wrap in Puff Pastry:
    - Preheat your oven to 400°F (200°C).
    - Roll out the puff pastry on a lightly floured surface.
    - Cut the pastry into two rectangles large enough to wrap each steak.

- Unwrap the steaks from the plastic wrap and place them in the center of the pastry rectangles.
- Fold the pastry over the steaks, sealing the edges with beaten egg. Trim any excess pastry.

5. Bake:
   - Place the wrapped steaks seam-side down on a baking sheet lined with parchment paper.
   - Brush the tops with beaten egg and water mixture.
   - Use a sharp knife to score the tops lightly.
   - Bake for 20-25 minutes until the pastry is golden brown.
6. Serve:
   - Let the Beef Wellingtons rest for 5 minutes before slicing.
   - Serve with your choice of sides and enjoy your romantic dinner!

Enjoy your elegant Beef Wellington dinner!

Chicken Marsala

Ingredients:

- 2 beef fillet steaks (about 6 oz each)
- Salt and freshly ground black pepper, to taste
- 2 tablespoons olive oil
- 1 tablespoon Dijon mustard
- 1 tablespoon unsalted butter
- 1 shallot, finely chopped
- 2 cloves garlic, minced
- 8 oz cremini mushrooms, finely chopped
- 1 tablespoon fresh thyme leaves
- 1/4 cup dry white wine
- 4 slices prosciutto
- 1 sheet puff pastry, thawed
- 1 egg, beaten
- 1 tablespoon water

Instructions:

1. Prepare the Steaks:
    - Season the beef fillets with salt and pepper.
    - Heat the olive oil in a pan over high heat.
    - Sear the steaks for 1-2 minutes on each side until browned. Remove from pan and let cool.
    - Brush the Dijon mustard over the cooled steaks.
2. Make the Duxelles:
    - In the same pan, melt the butter over medium heat.
    - Add the shallot and garlic, cooking until softened, about 2-3 minutes.
    - Add the chopped mushrooms and thyme, cooking until the mushrooms release their moisture and become dry.
    - Pour in the white wine and cook until evaporated. Season with salt and pepper, and let cool.
3. Assemble the Wellington:
    - Lay a sheet of plastic wrap on a work surface.
    - Arrange the prosciutto slices in a layer, overlapping slightly.
    - Spread half of the mushroom mixture over the prosciutto.
    - Place one steak in the center and wrap the prosciutto around it using the plastic wrap to form a tight bundle. Repeat with the other steak. Refrigerate for 15-20 minutes.
4. Wrap in Puff Pastry:
    - Preheat your oven to 400°F (200°C).
    - Roll out the puff pastry on a lightly floured surface.
    - Cut the pastry into two rectangles large enough to wrap each steak.

- Unwrap the steaks from the plastic wrap and place them in the center of the pastry rectangles.
- Fold the pastry over the steaks, sealing the edges with beaten egg. Trim any excess pastry.

5. **Bake:**
   - Place the wrapped steaks seam-side down on a baking sheet lined with parchment paper.
   - Brush the tops with beaten egg and water mixture.
   - Use a sharp knife to score the tops lightly.
   - Bake for 20-25 minutes until the pastry is golden brown.

6. **Serve:**
   - Let the Beef Wellingtons rest for 5 minutes before slicing.
   - Serve with your choice of sides and enjoy your romantic dinner!

Enjoy your elegant Beef Wellington dinner!

Chicken Marsala

Ingredients:

- 2 boneless, skinless chicken breasts
- Salt and freshly ground black pepper, to taste
- 1/2 cup all-purpose flour
- 2 tablespoons olive oil
- 3 tablespoons unsalted butter, divided
- 1 shallot, finely chopped
- 2 cloves garlic, minced
- 8 oz cremini mushrooms, sliced
- 1/2 cup Marsala wine
- 1/2 cup chicken broth
- 1/4 cup heavy cream (optional)
- 1 tablespoon chopped fresh parsley

Instructions:

1. Prepare the Chicken:
    - Pound the chicken breasts to an even thickness, about 1/2 inch.
    - Season with salt and pepper.
    - Dredge the chicken in the flour, shaking off any excess.
2. Cook the Chicken:
    - In a large skillet, heat the olive oil and 1 tablespoon of butter over medium-high heat.
    - Add the chicken breasts and cook for 4-5 minutes per side, until golden brown and cooked through. Remove from the pan and set aside.
3. Make the Sauce:
    - In the same skillet, add another tablespoon of butter.
    - Sauté the shallot and garlic until softened, about 2-3 minutes.
    - Add the mushrooms and cook until they release their moisture and become golden, about 5-7 minutes.
4. Deglaze and Simmer:
    - Pour in the Marsala wine, scraping up any browned bits from the bottom of the pan.
    - Let the wine simmer and reduce by half.
    - Add the chicken broth and bring to a simmer.
    - Stir in the remaining tablespoon of butter and heavy cream (if using).
5. Combine and Serve:
    - Return the chicken breasts to the skillet, spooning some sauce over them.
    - Let the chicken simmer in the sauce for a few minutes to absorb the flavors.
    - Sprinkle with chopped fresh parsley before serving.

Enjoy your delicious Chicken Marsala dinner!

Shrimp Scampi

Ingredients:

- 8 oz linguine or spaghetti
- 1/2 lb large shrimp, peeled and deveined
- Salt and freshly ground black pepper, to taste
- 2 tablespoons olive oil
- 3 tablespoons unsalted butter, divided
- 4 cloves garlic, minced
- 1/4 teaspoon red pepper flakes (optional)
- 1/2 cup dry white wine
- 1 tablespoon fresh lemon juice
- 1/4 cup chopped fresh parsley
- Lemon wedges, for serving

Instructions:

1. Cook the Pasta:
    - Bring a large pot of salted water to a boil.
    - Cook the linguine or spaghetti according to the package instructions until al dente.
    - Drain and set aside.
2. Prepare the Shrimp:
    - Season the shrimp with salt and pepper.
    - In a large skillet, heat the olive oil and 2 tablespoons of butter over medium-high heat.
    - Add the shrimp and cook for 2-3 minutes on each side until pink and opaque.
    - Remove the shrimp from the skillet and set aside.
3. Make the Sauce:
    - In the same skillet, add the remaining 1 tablespoon of butter.
    - Sauté the garlic and red pepper flakes (if using) until fragrant, about 1 minute.
    - Pour in the white wine and lemon juice, scraping up any browned bits from the bottom of the pan.
    - Let the sauce simmer and reduce by half.
4. Combine and Serve:
    - Return the cooked shrimp to the skillet and toss to coat in the sauce.
    - Add the cooked pasta to the skillet and toss to combine.
    - Sprinkle with chopped fresh parsley.
    - Serve immediately with lemon wedges on the side.

Enjoy your flavorful Shrimp Scampi dinner!

Filet Mignon

Ingredients:

- 2 (6-8 oz) filet mignon steaks
- Salt and freshly ground black pepper, to taste
- 2 tablespoons olive oil
- 2 tablespoons unsalted butter
- 2 cloves garlic, crushed
- 2 sprigs fresh rosemary
- 1/2 cup beef broth
- 1/2 cup dry red wine
- 1 tablespoon Dijon mustard
- 1 tablespoon chopped fresh parsley

Instructions:

1. Prepare the Steaks:
    - Let the steaks come to room temperature for about 30 minutes.
    - Preheat your oven to 400°F (200°C).
    - Season the steaks generously with salt and freshly ground black pepper on both sides.
2. Sear the Steaks:
    - In a large oven-safe skillet, heat the olive oil over medium-high heat until hot.
    - Add the steaks and sear for 2-3 minutes on each side until a brown crust forms.
    - Add the butter, garlic, and rosemary to the skillet.
3. Roast the Steaks:
    - Transfer the skillet to the preheated oven.
    - Roast the steaks for about 5-7 minutes for medium-rare, or until they reach your desired level of doneness (use a meat thermometer for accuracy: 130-135°F for medium-rare).
    - Remove the steaks from the oven and transfer to a plate. Tent with foil and let rest.
4. Make the Sauce:
    - Discard the rosemary and garlic from the skillet.
    - Place the skillet back on the stovetop over medium heat.
    - Add the beef broth and red wine, scraping up any browned bits from the bottom of the pan.
    - Let the mixture simmer and reduce by half.
    - Stir in the Dijon mustard and continue to simmer until the sauce thickens slightly.
    - Season with salt and pepper to taste.
5. Serve:
    - Plate the rested steaks and spoon the sauce over the top.
    - Garnish with chopped fresh parsley.
    - Serve immediately with your choice of sides.

Enjoy your elegant Filet Mignon dinner!

Duck à l'Orange

Ingredients:

- 2 duck breasts
- Salt and freshly ground black pepper, to taste
- 1/2 cup orange juice (freshly squeezed is best)
- 1/2 cup chicken broth
- 1/4 cup Grand Marnier or other orange liqueur
- 1 tablespoon honey
- 1 tablespoon white wine vinegar
- 1 orange, segmented
- 1 teaspoon orange zest
- 1 tablespoon unsalted butter
- Fresh thyme, for garnish

Instructions:

1. Prepare the Duck Breasts:
   - Score the skin of the duck breasts in a crisscross pattern, being careful not to cut into the meat.
   - Season both sides with salt and freshly ground black pepper.
2. Sear the Duck Breasts:
   - Place the duck breasts skin-side down in a cold, non-stick skillet.
   - Turn the heat to medium and cook for about 8-10 minutes, until the skin is crispy and most of the fat has rendered.
   - Flip the duck breasts and cook for another 3-4 minutes for medium-rare, or longer if desired.
   - Remove the duck breasts from the skillet and let them rest, tented with foil.
3. Make the Orange Sauce:
   - Pour off most of the duck fat from the skillet, leaving about 1 tablespoon.
   - Add the orange juice, chicken broth, Grand Marnier, honey, and white wine vinegar to the skillet.
   - Bring to a simmer, scraping up any browned bits from the bottom of the pan.
   - Let the sauce reduce by half, about 10 minutes.
4. Finish the Sauce:
   - Stir in the orange segments and orange zest.
   - Add the butter and stir until melted and the sauce is glossy.
   - Season with salt and pepper to taste.
5. Serve:
   - Slice the duck breasts and arrange them on plates.
   - Spoon the orange sauce over the duck.
   - Garnish with fresh thyme.

Enjoy your exquisite Duck à l'Orange dinner!

Coq au Vin

Ingredients:

- 2 bone-in, skin-on chicken thighs
- 2 bone-in, skin-on chicken drumsticks
- Salt and freshly ground black pepper, to taste
- 2 tablespoons olive oil
- 4 oz bacon, diced
- 1 small onion, chopped
- 2 cloves garlic, minced
- 1 carrot, sliced
- 1 celery stalk, sliced
- 1 tablespoon tomato paste
- 1 tablespoon all-purpose flour
- 1 cup red wine (such as Burgundy or Pinot Noir)
- 1/2 cup chicken broth
- 1 bay leaf
- 2 sprigs fresh thyme
- 8 oz cremini mushrooms, sliced
- 1 tablespoon unsalted butter
- Fresh parsley, chopped (for garnish)

Instructions:

1. Prepare the Chicken:
    - Season the chicken thighs and drumsticks with salt and pepper.
    - In a large, heavy-bottomed pot or Dutch oven, heat the olive oil over medium-high heat.
2. Brown the Chicken:
    - Add the chicken pieces to the pot, skin-side down, and brown for about 5-7 minutes per side until golden.
    - Remove the chicken from the pot and set aside.
3. Cook the Bacon and Vegetables:
    - Add the diced bacon to the pot and cook until crispy.
    - Remove the bacon with a slotted spoon and set aside, leaving the fat in the pot.
    - Add the chopped onion, garlic, carrot, and celery to the pot.
    - Sauté until the vegetables are softened, about 5 minutes.
4. Add Tomato Paste and Flour:
    - Stir in the tomato paste and cook for 1 minute.
    - Sprinkle the flour over the vegetables and stir well to combine. Cook for another 2 minutes.
5. Deglaze and Simmer:
    - Pour in the red wine, scraping up any browned bits from the bottom of the pot.
    - Add the chicken broth, bay leaf, and thyme sprigs.

- Return the chicken and bacon to the pot.
    - Bring to a simmer, then reduce the heat to low, cover, and cook for 45 minutes, or until the chicken is tender and cooked through.
6. Cook the Mushrooms:
    - In a separate skillet, melt the butter over medium heat.
    - Add the sliced mushrooms and cook until they release their moisture and are golden brown.
    - Season with salt and pepper, then add the mushrooms to the pot with the chicken.
7. Finish and Serve:
    - Remove the bay leaf and thyme sprigs from the pot.
    - Adjust seasoning with salt and pepper if needed.
    - Serve the Coq au Vin in bowls, garnished with fresh parsley.

Enjoy your classic French Coq au Vin dinner!

Veal Saltimbocca

Ingredients:

- 2 veal escalopes (about 4 ounces each), pounded thin
- Salt and freshly ground black pepper
- 4 slices prosciutto
- 8 fresh sage leaves
- All-purpose flour, for dredging
- 2 tablespoons unsalted butter
- 2 tablespoons olive oil
- 1/4 cup dry white wine
- 1/4 cup chicken broth
- 1 tablespoon lemon juice
- Lemon wedges, for serving

Instructions:

1. Prepare the Veal:
    - Season the veal escalopes with salt and pepper on both sides.
    - Place a slice of prosciutto on each escalope, covering as much surface area as possible.
    - Place 2 sage leaves on top of the prosciutto on each escalope.
    - Secure the prosciutto and sage in place by gently pressing them onto the veal.
2. Dredge the Veal:
    - Dredge each veal escalope in flour, shaking off any excess.
3. Cook the Veal:
    - In a large skillet, heat the olive oil and butter over medium-high heat.
    - Once hot, add the veal escalopes to the skillet, prosciutto-side down.
    - Cook for about 2-3 minutes on each side, until the veal is golden brown and cooked through.
    - Transfer the cooked veal to a plate and cover with foil to keep warm.
4. Make the Sauce:
    - Deglaze the skillet with white wine, scraping up any browned bits from the bottom of the pan.
    - Add the chicken broth and lemon juice to the skillet.
    - Let the sauce simmer for a few minutes to reduce slightly.
5. Serve:
    - Place the veal escalopes on serving plates.
    - Spoon the sauce over the veal.
    - Garnish with additional fresh sage leaves and lemon wedges.
    - Serve immediately, accompanied by your favorite side dishes.

Enjoy your delicious Veal Saltimbocca dinner!

Stuffed Chicken Breast

Ingredients:

- 2 boneless, skinless chicken breasts
- Salt and freshly ground black pepper, to taste
- 1/2 cup baby spinach leaves
- 1/4 cup sun-dried tomatoes, chopped
- 1/4 cup feta cheese, crumbled
- 2 tablespoons olive oil
- 2 cloves garlic, minced
- 1 teaspoon dried Italian seasoning (or a mixture of dried basil, oregano, and thyme)
- 1/4 cup chicken broth or white wine (optional)
- Fresh parsley, chopped (for garnish)

Instructions:

1. Prepare the Chicken:
    - Preheat your oven to 375°F (190°C).
    - Place each chicken breast between two sheets of plastic wrap or parchment paper. Using a meat mallet or rolling pin, gently pound the chicken to an even thickness, about 1/2 inch thick.
    - Season both sides of the chicken breasts with salt and pepper.
2. Prepare the Filling:
    - In a small bowl, combine the baby spinach, chopped sun-dried tomatoes, and crumbled feta cheese.
3. Stuff the Chicken:
    - Lay the chicken breasts flat on a clean surface.
    - Spoon the spinach, sun-dried tomato, and feta mixture onto the center of each chicken breast.
    - Roll up the chicken breasts, enclosing the filling, and secure with toothpicks if needed.
4. Cook the Chicken:
    - In an oven-safe skillet, heat the olive oil over medium-high heat.
    - Add the minced garlic and Italian seasoning to the skillet and cook until fragrant, about 1 minute.
    - Carefully add the stuffed chicken breasts to the skillet, seam-side down.
    - Cook for 2-3 minutes on each side until golden brown.
    - If using, pour the chicken broth or white wine into the skillet around the chicken breasts.
5. Bake:
    - Transfer the skillet to the preheated oven.
    - Bake for 15-20 minutes, or until the chicken is cooked through and no longer pink in the center.
6. Serve:

- Remove the toothpicks from the chicken breasts.
- Garnish with fresh chopped parsley.
- Serve the stuffed chicken breasts hot, with your favorite side dishes.

Enjoy your flavorful Stuffed Chicken Breast dinner!

Grilled Lamb Chops

Ingredients:

- 4 lamb loin chops, about 1 inch thick
- Salt and freshly ground black pepper, to taste
- 2 cloves garlic, minced
- 1 tablespoon fresh rosemary leaves, chopped
- 1 tablespoon fresh thyme leaves, chopped
- 2 tablespoons olive oil
- 1 tablespoon lemon juice
- Lemon wedges, for serving
- Fresh parsley, chopped (for garnish)

Instructions:

1. Marinate the Lamb Chops:
    - In a shallow dish or resealable plastic bag, combine the minced garlic, chopped rosemary, chopped thyme, olive oil, and lemon juice.
    - Season the lamb chops generously with salt and pepper.
    - Add the lamb chops to the marinade, turning to coat evenly.
    - Cover the dish or seal the bag, and refrigerate for at least 30 minutes, or up to 4 hours, to allow the flavors to meld.
2. Preheat the Grill:
    - Preheat your grill to medium-high heat (about 375-400°F or 190-200°C).
3. Grill the Lamb Chops:
    - Remove the lamb chops from the marinade and discard any excess marinade.
    - Place the lamb chops on the preheated grill.
    - Grill for about 3-4 minutes on each side for medium-rare, or adjust cooking time according to your desired level of doneness.
4. Rest and Serve:
    - Remove the lamb chops from the grill and transfer to a plate.
    - Tent the lamb chops loosely with foil and let them rest for 5 minutes to allow the juices to redistribute.
5. Serve:
    - Arrange the grilled lamb chops on serving plates.
    - Garnish with chopped fresh parsley and serve with lemon wedges on the side.

Enjoy your succulent Grilled Lamb Chops!

Seafood Paella

Ingredients:

- 1/2 cup Arborio rice
- 1 1/2 cups chicken or seafood broth
- 4-6 large shrimp, peeled and deveined
- 4-6 mussels, cleaned and debearded
- 4-6 clams, scrubbed
- 1/4 cup diced onion
- 1/4 cup diced bell pepper (red or green)
- 2 cloves garlic, minced
- 1 ripe tomato, diced
- 1/4 cup frozen peas
- 1/4 teaspoon smoked paprika
- 1/4 teaspoon saffron threads
- Salt and pepper to taste
- 2 tablespoons olive oil
- Lemon wedges, for serving
- Fresh parsley, chopped (for garnish)

Instructions:

1. Prepare the Saffron Broth:
    - In a small saucepan, heat the chicken or seafood broth until warm. Add the saffron threads and let them steep in the broth for at least 10 minutes to infuse the flavor and color.
2. Prepare the Seafood:
    - Season the shrimp with salt, pepper, and a pinch of smoked paprika.
    - In a separate skillet, heat 1 tablespoon of olive oil over medium-high heat.
    - Add the shrimp and cook for 1-2 minutes on each side until pink and cooked through. Remove from the skillet and set aside.
    - In the same skillet, add the clams and mussels. Pour in a splash of water or white wine, cover, and cook for 3-4 minutes until the shells open. Discard any shells that do not open. Remove the seafood from the shells and set aside.
3. Cook the Paella:
    - In a large skillet or paella pan, heat the remaining 1 tablespoon of olive oil over medium heat.
    - Add the diced onion and bell pepper to the skillet and cook until softened, about 3-4 minutes.
    - Stir in the minced garlic and cook for an additional 1 minute until fragrant.
    - Add the diced tomato and cook for 2-3 minutes until it starts to break down.
    - Stir in the Arborio rice and cook for 1-2 minutes until lightly toasted.
    - Pour in the saffron-infused broth, along with any remaining broth from cooking the seafood. Season with salt, pepper, and smoked paprika.

        - Arrange the cooked shrimp, clams, mussels, and frozen peas on top of the rice.
4. Simmer and Serve:
    - Reduce the heat to low and cover the skillet with a lid or aluminum foil. Let the paella simmer for 15-20 minutes, or until the rice is cooked and has absorbed the liquid.
    - Once the rice is cooked, remove the skillet from the heat and let it rest, covered, for 5 minutes.
    - Garnish with chopped fresh parsley and serve hot with lemon wedges on the side.

Enjoy your flavorful Seafood Paella for Two!

Osso Buco

Ingredients:

- 2 pieces of veal shank (about 1 inch thick)
- Salt and freshly ground black pepper
- All-purpose flour, for dredging
- 2 tablespoons olive oil
- 1 tablespoon unsalted butter
- 1 small onion, finely chopped
- 1 carrot, finely chopped
- 1 celery stalk, finely chopped
- 2 cloves garlic, minced
- 1/2 cup dry white wine
- 1 cup canned diced tomatoes
- 1 cup beef or chicken broth
- 1 bay leaf
- 1 sprig fresh rosemary
- 1 sprig fresh thyme
- Zest of 1 lemon
- Gremolata (optional, for serving)
    - 2 tablespoons chopped fresh parsley
    - 1 garlic clove, minced
    - Zest of 1 lemon

Instructions:

1. Prepare the Veal Shank:
    - Season the veal shanks generously with salt and pepper.
    - Dredge the shanks in flour, shaking off any excess.
2. Brown the Veal Shank:
    - In a large, heavy-bottomed skillet or Dutch oven, heat the olive oil and butter over medium-high heat.
    - Add the veal shanks to the skillet and brown them on all sides, about 4-5 minutes per side. Remove from the skillet and set aside.
3. Cook the Aromatics:
    - In the same skillet, add the chopped onion, carrot, celery, and minced garlic.
    - Cook, stirring occasionally, until the vegetables are softened, about 5-7 minutes.
4. Deglaze the Pan:
    - Pour in the white wine and scrape up any browned bits from the bottom of the skillet.
    - Let the wine simmer and reduce by half.
5. Simmer the Osso Buco:
    - Return the browned veal shanks to the skillet.

- Add the diced tomatoes, beef or chicken broth, bay leaf, rosemary, thyme, and lemon zest to the skillet.
    - Bring the mixture to a simmer, then reduce the heat to low.
    - Cover the skillet and let the osso buco simmer gently for about 1 1/2 to 2 hours, or until the meat is tender and falling off the bone.
6. Prepare the Gremolata (Optional):
    - In a small bowl, combine the chopped fresh parsley, minced garlic, and lemon zest. Set aside.
7. Serve:
    - Once the osso buco is cooked, remove the bay leaf, rosemary, and thyme sprigs.
    - Serve the osso buco hot, with the sauce spooned over the top.
    - Garnish with the optional gremolata, if desired.

Enjoy your delicious Osso Buco for Two!

Rack of Lamb

Ingredients:

- 1 rack of lamb, trimmed and frenched (about 1 to 1.5 pounds)
- Salt and freshly ground black pepper
- 2 cloves garlic, minced
- 1 tablespoon fresh rosemary leaves, chopped
- 1 tablespoon fresh thyme leaves, chopped
- 2 tablespoons olive oil
- 1 tablespoon Dijon mustard
- 1 tablespoon balsamic vinegar
- 1 tablespoon honey
- 1/4 cup breadcrumbs (optional, for crust)

Instructions:

1. Prepare the Rack of Lamb:
    - Preheat your oven to 400°F (200°C).
    - Season the rack of lamb generously with salt and pepper on both sides.
2. Make the Herb Crust (Optional):
    - In a small bowl, combine the minced garlic, chopped rosemary, chopped thyme, olive oil, and breadcrumbs (if using).
    - Mix well to form a paste.
3. Coat the Lamb:
    - In another small bowl, whisk together the Dijon mustard, balsamic vinegar, and honey.
    - Brush the mustard mixture over the rack of lamb, coating it evenly on all sides.
4. Cook the Lamb:
    - Heat an oven-safe skillet over high heat.
    - Once hot, sear the rack of lamb, fat-side down, for about 2-3 minutes until browned.
    - Turn the rack of lamb over and sear the other side for an additional 2-3 minutes.
5. Finish in the Oven:
    - If using the herb crust, spread it evenly over the seared rack of lamb.
    - Transfer the skillet to the preheated oven.
    - Roast the rack of lamb in the oven for 15-20 minutes for medium-rare, or until it reaches your desired level of doneness (use a meat thermometer for accuracy: 130-135°F for medium-rare).
    - Remove the rack of lamb from the oven and let it rest for 5-10 minutes before slicing.
6. Slice and Serve:
    - Slice the rack of lamb between the bones into individual chops.
    - Arrange the lamb chops on serving plates.
    - Serve hot, accompanied by your favorite side dishes.

Enjoy your elegant Rack of Lamb for Two!

Chateaubriand

Ingredients:

- 1 Chateaubriand beef tenderloin roast (about 1 1/2 to 2 pounds)
- Salt and freshly ground black pepper
- 2 tablespoons olive oil
- 2 tablespoons unsalted butter
- 4 cloves garlic, smashed
- 2 sprigs fresh rosemary
- 2 sprigs fresh thyme
- Optional: Red wine reduction or béarnaise sauce for serving

Instructions:

1. Preheat the Oven:
    - Preheat your oven to 400°F (200°C).
2. Prepare the Chateaubriand:
    - Season the Chateaubriand generously with salt and pepper on all sides.
3. Sear the Chateaubriand:
    - In an oven-safe skillet or cast-iron pan, heat the olive oil over high heat.
    - Once hot, add the Chateaubriand to the skillet and sear it on all sides until browned, about 2-3 minutes per side.
4. Add Aromatics:
    - Add the smashed garlic cloves, rosemary sprigs, and thyme sprigs to the skillet.
    - Add the butter to the skillet and baste the Chateaubriand with the melted butter and aromatics.
5. Roast the Chateaubriand:
    - Transfer the skillet to the preheated oven.
    - Roast the Chateaubriand in the oven for about 15-20 minutes, or until it reaches your desired level of doneness (use a meat thermometer for accuracy: 125°F for rare, 135°F for medium-rare, 145°F for medium).
6. Rest and Serve:
    - Once cooked to your liking, remove the skillet from the oven.
    - Transfer the Chateaubriand to a cutting board and let it rest for 10 minutes before slicing.
7. Slice and Serve:
    - Slice the Chateaubriand into thick slices.
    - Serve the sliced Chateaubriand hot, accompanied by your choice of sauce such as red wine reduction or béarnaise sauce.

Enjoy your exquisite Chateaubriand for Two!

Bouillabaisse

Ingredients:

For the Broth:

- 2 cups fish or seafood stock
- 1 cup water
- 1 onion, chopped
- 2 cloves garlic, minced
- 1 celery stalk, chopped
- 1 carrot, chopped
- 1 bay leaf
- 2 sprigs fresh thyme
- 1/2 teaspoon saffron threads
- Salt and pepper to taste

For the Bouillabaisse:

- 8 oz white fish fillets (such as cod or halibut), cut into chunks
- 8 oz shrimp, peeled and deveined
- 4 oz mussels, scrubbed and debearded
- 4 oz clams, scrubbed
- 1/2 cup dry white wine
- 1 tablespoon olive oil
- 1 small onion, finely chopped
- 2 cloves garlic, minced
- 1 red bell pepper, sliced
- 1 small fennel bulb, sliced
- 1 large tomato, diced
- 2 tablespoons tomato paste
- Salt and pepper to taste
- Fresh parsley, chopped (for garnish)
- Crusty bread, for serving

Instructions:

1. Prepare the Broth:
    - In a large pot, combine the fish or seafood stock, water, chopped onion, minced garlic, chopped celery, chopped carrot, bay leaf, thyme sprigs, and saffron threads.
    - Season with salt and pepper to taste.
    - Bring the broth to a boil, then reduce the heat and let it simmer for about 30 minutes to develop the flavors.
2. Prepare the Seafood:

- In a separate pot, bring the white wine to a boil.
- Add the mussels and clams to the pot, cover, and cook for about 5 minutes, or until the shells open. Discard any unopened shells.
- Remove the mussels and clams from the pot and set aside.
- Strain the cooking liquid through a fine-mesh sieve lined with cheesecloth to remove any grit. Set aside.

3. Cook the Bouillabaisse:
   - In the same pot used for the seafood broth, heat the olive oil over medium heat.
   - Add the finely chopped onion and minced garlic to the pot and cook until softened, about 3-4 minutes.
   - Add the sliced red bell pepper and sliced fennel bulb to the pot and cook for an additional 5 minutes until softened.
   - Stir in the diced tomato and tomato paste, and cook for another 3-4 minutes.
   - Pour in the strained cooking liquid from the mussels and clams, along with the prepared fish or seafood broth.
   - Bring the mixture to a simmer and let it cook for about 10-15 minutes to blend the flavors.

4. Add the Seafood:
   - Add the chunks of white fish fillets, peeled shrimp, cooked mussels, and cooked clams to the pot.
   - Let the seafood simmer gently in the broth for about 5-7 minutes, or until the fish is cooked through and the shrimp turns pink.

5. Serve:
   - Ladle the bouillabaisse into serving bowls.
   - Garnish with chopped fresh parsley.
   - Serve hot with crusty bread on the side.

Enjoy your delightful Bouillabaisse for Two!

Seared Scallops

Ingredients:

- 6 large sea scallops, patted dry
- Salt and pepper to taste
- 1 tablespoon olive oil
- 1 tablespoon unsalted butter
- Lemon wedges, for serving
- Fresh parsley, chopped (for garnish, optional)

Instructions:

1. Prepare the Scallops:
    - Ensure the scallops are dry by patting them with paper towels. Moisture prevents proper searing.
    - Season both sides of the scallops generously with salt and pepper.
2. Heat the Pan:
    - Heat a skillet (preferably non-stick or cast iron) over medium-high heat. Ensure the pan is hot before adding the scallops.
3. Sear the Scallops:
    - Add the olive oil to the hot skillet, followed by the butter.
    - Once the butter has melted and is sizzling, add the scallops to the skillet, making sure they are not crowded. Leave space between each scallop to ensure even cooking and browning.
    - Sear the scallops without moving them for about 2-3 minutes on one side until they develop a golden crust. Avoid the temptation to move or flip them too soon, as this can inhibit proper caramelization.
    - Flip the scallops using tongs and sear for an additional 2-3 minutes on the other side. The scallops should be opaque and slightly firm to the touch when cooked through.
4. Serve:
    - Transfer the seared scallops to a serving plate.
    - Garnish with chopped fresh parsley, if desired.
    - Serve immediately with lemon wedges on the side for squeezing over the scallops.

Enjoy your perfectly seared scallops for two!

Eggplant Parmesan

Ingredients:

- 1 medium eggplant, sliced into 1/4-inch rounds
- Salt
- 1 cup breadcrumbs
- 1/2 cup grated Parmesan cheese
- 2 eggs, beaten
- Olive oil, for frying
- 1 1/2 cups marinara sauce
- 1 cup shredded mozzarella cheese
- Fresh basil leaves, torn, for garnish (optional)

Instructions:

1. Preheat the Oven:
    - Preheat your oven to 375°F (190°C).
2. Prepare the Eggplant:
    - Place the eggplant slices on a paper towel-lined baking sheet.
    - Sprinkle both sides of the eggplant slices with salt and let them sit for about 15-20 minutes. This helps to draw out excess moisture and bitterness from the eggplant.
    - After 20 minutes, pat the eggplant slices dry with paper towels to remove the excess moisture.
3. Bread the Eggplant:
    - In a shallow dish, combine the breadcrumbs and grated Parmesan cheese.
    - Dip each eggplant slice into the beaten eggs, then coat it in the breadcrumb mixture, pressing gently to adhere.
4. Fry the Eggplant:
    - In a large skillet, heat about 1/4 inch of olive oil over medium heat.
    - Once the oil is hot, add the breaded eggplant slices in batches, being careful not to overcrowd the skillet.
    - Fry the eggplant slices for about 2-3 minutes on each side, or until golden brown and crispy.
    - Transfer the fried eggplant slices to a paper towel-lined plate to drain any excess oil.
5. Assemble the Eggplant Parmesan:
    - Spread a thin layer of marinara sauce on the bottom of a baking dish.
    - Arrange half of the fried eggplant slices in a single layer over the sauce.
    - Spoon more marinara sauce over the eggplant slices.
    - Sprinkle half of the shredded mozzarella cheese over the sauce.
    - Repeat the layers with the remaining eggplant slices, marinara sauce, and shredded mozzarella cheese.
6. Bake:

- Cover the baking dish with aluminum foil and bake in the preheated oven for 20-25 minutes, or until the cheese is melted and bubbly.
7. Serve:
    - Remove the foil from the baking dish and bake for an additional 5 minutes, or until the cheese is golden brown.
    - Garnish with torn fresh basil leaves, if desired.
    - Serve the Eggplant Parmesan hot, with crusty bread or pasta on the side.

Enjoy your delicious Eggplant Parmesan for Two!

Chicken Piccata

Ingredients:

- 2 boneless, skinless chicken breasts
- Salt and pepper, to taste
- All-purpose flour, for dredging
- 2 tablespoons unsalted butter
- 2 tablespoons olive oil
- 2 cloves garlic, minced
- 1/4 cup white wine (such as dry vermouth or chicken broth)
- 1/2 cup chicken broth
- 2 tablespoons freshly squeezed lemon juice
- 2 tablespoons capers, drained
- 2 tablespoons chopped fresh parsley, for garnish
- Lemon slices, for serving

Instructions:

1. Prepare the Chicken:
    - Place each chicken breast between two sheets of plastic wrap or parchment paper. Using a meat mallet or rolling pin, gently pound the chicken to an even thickness, about 1/2 inch thick.
    - Season both sides of the chicken breasts with salt and pepper.
    - Dredge the chicken breasts in flour, shaking off any excess.
2. Cook the Chicken:
    - In a large skillet, heat 1 tablespoon of butter and 1 tablespoon of olive oil over medium-high heat.
    - Once the butter has melted and the oil is hot, add the chicken breasts to the skillet.
    - Cook the chicken for about 3-4 minutes on each side until golden brown and cooked through. Remove the chicken from the skillet and set aside.
3. Make the Piccata Sauce:
    - In the same skillet, add the remaining tablespoon of butter and olive oil.
    - Add the minced garlic to the skillet and cook for about 1 minute until fragrant.
    - Deglaze the skillet with white wine, scraping up any browned bits from the bottom of the pan.
    - Let the wine simmer for about 1-2 minutes to reduce slightly.
    - Stir in the chicken broth, lemon juice, and capers. Bring the sauce to a simmer.
4. Finish and Serve:
    - Return the cooked chicken breasts to the skillet, turning to coat them in the sauce.
    - Simmer the chicken in the sauce for another 2-3 minutes to heat through and allow the flavors to meld.
    - Garnish with chopped fresh parsley.

- Serve the Chicken Piccata hot, with lemon slices on the side for squeezing over the chicken.

Enjoy your flavorful Chicken Piccata for Two!

Salmon en Croûte

Ingredients:

- 2 salmon fillets (6-8 ounces each), skinless
- Salt and pepper, to taste
- 1 sheet puff pastry, thawed according to package instructions
- 1 tablespoon Dijon mustard
- 1 tablespoon honey
- 1/4 cup breadcrumbs
- 1 egg, beaten (for egg wash)
- Fresh dill, chopped (for garnish, optional)

Instructions:

1. Prepare the Salmon:
    - Preheat your oven to 400°F (200°C).
    - Season the salmon fillets with salt and pepper on both sides.
2. Roll Out Puff Pastry:
    - On a lightly floured surface, roll out the puff pastry sheet to a rectangle large enough to wrap around both salmon fillets.
3. Assemble the Salmon en Croûte:
    - In a small bowl, mix together the Dijon mustard and honey.
    - Spread the mustard-honey mixture evenly over the top of each salmon fillet.
    - Sprinkle breadcrumbs over the mustard-honey mixture.
4. Wrap in Puff Pastry:
    - Place each salmon fillet in the center of the puff pastry sheet.
    - Fold the pastry over the salmon, sealing the edges by pressing with your fingers or using a fork.
    - Trim any excess pastry if necessary.
5. Brush with Egg Wash:
    - Transfer the wrapped salmon fillets to a baking sheet lined with parchment paper.
    - Brush the top and sides of the puff pastry with beaten egg, ensuring it is evenly coated.
6. Bake:
    - Bake the salmon en croûte in the preheated oven for 20-25 minutes, or until the pastry is golden brown and crispy.
7. Serve:
    - Remove from the oven and let it rest for a few minutes.
    - Garnish with chopped fresh dill, if desired.
    - Slice and serve the Salmon en Croûte hot, accompanied by your favorite side dishes.

Enjoy your delicious Salmon en Croûte for Two!

Pork Tenderloin with Apple Cider Reduction

Ingredients:

- 1 pork tenderloin (about 1 pound)
- Salt and pepper, to taste
- 1 tablespoon olive oil
- 1 tablespoon unsalted butter
- 1/2 cup apple cider or apple juice
- 1/4 cup chicken broth
- 1 tablespoon Dijon mustard
- 1 tablespoon honey or maple syrup
- 1/2 teaspoon dried thyme (or 1 teaspoon fresh thyme leaves)
- 1/4 cup heavy cream (optional, for richness)

Instructions:

1. Prepare the Pork Tenderloin:
   - Preheat your oven to 400°F (200°C).
   - Season the pork tenderloin with salt and pepper on all sides.
2. Sear the Pork Tenderloin:
   - In an oven-safe skillet, heat the olive oil and butter over medium-high heat.
   - Once hot, add the pork tenderloin to the skillet and sear it on all sides until browned, about 2-3 minutes per side.
3. Roast the Pork Tenderloin:
   - Transfer the skillet to the preheated oven.
   - Roast the pork tenderloin in the oven for about 15-20 minutes, or until it reaches an internal temperature of 145°F (63°C) for medium-rare or 160°F (71°C) for medium, using a meat thermometer inserted into the thickest part of the tenderloin.
   - Remove the pork from the oven and transfer it to a cutting board. Tent with foil and let it rest while you prepare the sauce.
4. Make the Apple Cider Reduction:
   - In the same skillet used to cook the pork (remove excess fat if necessary), add the apple cider or apple juice, chicken broth, Dijon mustard, honey or maple syrup, and dried thyme.
   - Bring the mixture to a boil over medium-high heat, scraping up any browned bits from the bottom of the skillet.
   - Let the sauce simmer and reduce until it thickens slightly, about 5-7 minutes.
   - If using, stir in the heavy cream and simmer for an additional 1-2 minutes until the sauce is smooth and slightly thickened.
5. Slice and Serve:
   - Slice the rested pork tenderloin into thick slices.
   - Serve the pork tenderloin slices drizzled with the apple cider reduction sauce.
   - Optionally, garnish with fresh thyme leaves or parsley.

- Serve hot, accompanied by roasted vegetables or mashed potatoes.

Enjoy your delicious Pork Tenderloin with Apple Cider Reduction for Two!

Baked Halibut with Herb Butter

Ingredients:

- 2 halibut fillets (6-8 ounces each)
- Salt and pepper, to taste
- 2 tablespoons unsalted butter, softened
- 1 tablespoon chopped fresh herbs (such as parsley, dill, and chives)
- 1 garlic clove, minced
- 1 tablespoon lemon juice
- 1/4 teaspoon lemon zest
- 1 tablespoon olive oil
- Lemon wedges, for serving
- Fresh herbs, for garnish

Instructions:

1. Preheat the Oven:
    - Preheat your oven to 400°F (200°C).
2. Prepare the Herb Butter:
    - In a small bowl, combine the softened butter, chopped fresh herbs, minced garlic, lemon juice, and lemon zest. Mix well until all ingredients are evenly incorporated.
3. Prepare the Halibut:
    - Pat the halibut fillets dry with paper towels.
    - Season both sides of the halibut fillets with salt and pepper.
4. Bake the Halibut:
    - Place the halibut fillets on a baking sheet lined with parchment paper or lightly greased.
    - Brush the top of each halibut fillet with olive oil.
    - Spread a generous amount of the herb butter mixture over the top of each fillet, covering evenly.
5. Bake in the Oven:
    - Bake the halibut fillets in the preheated oven for 12-15 minutes, or until the fish is opaque and flakes easily with a fork.
6. Serve:
    - Remove the halibut fillets from the oven and let them rest for a few minutes.
    - Garnish with additional fresh herbs and serve hot with lemon wedges on the side.

Enjoy your delicious Baked Halibut with Herb Butter for Two!

Risotto Milanese

Ingredients:

- 1 cup Arborio rice
- 4 cups chicken or vegetable broth
- 1/2 cup dry white wine
- 1 small onion, finely chopped
- 2 tablespoons unsalted butter
- 1 tablespoon olive oil
- 1/2 teaspoon saffron threads
- 1/2 cup grated Parmesan cheese, plus extra for serving
- Salt and pepper, to taste

Instructions:

1. Prepare the Saffron Infusion:
    - In a small bowl, combine the saffron threads with 2 tablespoons of warm water. Let it steep and infuse for about 10-15 minutes.
2. Prepare the Broth:
    - In a saucepan, heat the chicken or vegetable broth over low heat. Keep it warm throughout the cooking process.
3. Cook the Risotto:
    - In a large, heavy-bottomed skillet or pot, heat the olive oil and 1 tablespoon of butter over medium heat.
    - Add the chopped onion to the skillet and cook until translucent, about 3-4 minutes.
4. Toast the Rice:
    - Add the Arborio rice to the skillet and toast it for 1-2 minutes, stirring constantly, until the rice grains are coated with oil and slightly translucent.
5. Deglaze with Wine:
    - Pour in the white wine and stir continuously until the wine is absorbed by the rice.
6. Add the Broth:
    - Begin adding the warm broth to the rice mixture, one ladleful (about 1/2 cup) at a time.
    - Stir constantly and allow each addition of broth to be absorbed by the rice before adding the next ladleful.
    - Continue this process for about 18-20 minutes, or until the rice is creamy and cooked al dente. You may not need to use all of the broth.
7. Finish the Risotto:
    - Stir in the saffron infusion along with the remaining tablespoon of butter and grated Parmesan cheese.
    - Season with salt and pepper to taste. The risotto should be creamy and slightly runny (all'onda).
8. Serve:

- Remove the risotto from heat and let it rest for a minute or two.
- Serve the Risotto Milanese hot, garnished with extra grated Parmesan cheese if desired.

Enjoy your authentic and creamy Risotto Milanese for Two!

Beef Stroganoff

Ingredients:

- 1/2 pound beef sirloin or tenderloin, thinly sliced into strips
- Salt and pepper, to taste
- 1 tablespoon olive oil
- 2 tablespoons unsalted butter
- 1 small onion, finely chopped
- 2 cloves garlic, minced
- 8 oz mushrooms, sliced
- 1 tablespoon all-purpose flour
- 1/2 cup beef broth
- 1 tablespoon Dijon mustard
- 1 tablespoon Worcestershire sauce
- 1/2 cup sour cream
- Fresh parsley, chopped, for garnish
- Cooked egg noodles or rice, for serving

Instructions:

1. Prepare the Beef:
    - Season the beef strips with salt and pepper.
2. Cook the Beef:
    - In a large skillet, heat the olive oil over medium-high heat.
    - Add the beef strips and cook for 2-3 minutes per side until browned and cooked through.
    - Remove the beef from the skillet and set aside.
3. Make the Sauce:
    - In the same skillet, melt the butter over medium heat.
    - Add the chopped onion and cook until softened, about 3-4 minutes.
    - Add the minced garlic and sliced mushrooms to the skillet. Cook for another 4-5 minutes until the mushrooms are tender and browned.
4. Thicken the Sauce:
    - Sprinkle the flour over the mushroom mixture in the skillet. Stir well to combine and cook for 1 minute to cook off the raw flour taste.
5. Add the Liquid Ingredients:
    - Slowly pour in the beef broth, stirring constantly to incorporate the flour into the broth and prevent lumps from forming.
    - Stir in the Dijon mustard and Worcestershire sauce. Bring the mixture to a simmer and cook for 2-3 minutes until slightly thickened.
6. Finish the Dish:
    - Reduce the heat to low. Stir in the sour cream until smooth and well combined.
    - Return the cooked beef strips to the skillet and stir to coat them in the sauce. Cook for another 1-2 minutes until heated through.

7. **Serve:**
    - Serve the Beef Stroganoff hot over cooked egg noodles or rice.
    - Garnish with chopped fresh parsley.
    - Enjoy your delicious Beef Stroganoff for Two!

This recipe is rich, creamy, and comforting—a perfect meal for a cozy dinner for two.

Moroccan Lamb Tagine

Ingredients:

- 1 lb lamb shoulder or leg, cubed
- Salt and pepper, to taste
- 2 tablespoons olive oil
- 1 onion, finely chopped
- 2 cloves garlic, minced
- 1 teaspoon ground cumin
- 1 teaspoon ground coriander
- 1/2 teaspoon ground cinnamon
- 1/2 teaspoon ground ginger
- 1/4 teaspoon ground turmeric
- Pinch of saffron threads (optional)
- 1 tablespoon tomato paste
- 1 cup chicken broth or water
- 1 cup canned diced tomatoes, with juices
- 1 cup carrots, peeled and sliced
- 1 cup potatoes, peeled and diced
- 1/2 cup dried apricots, halved
- 1/4 cup golden raisins
- Zest of 1 lemon
- Fresh cilantro or parsley, chopped, for garnish
- Cooked couscous or rice, for serving

Instructions:

1. Prepare the Lamb:
    - Season the lamb cubes with salt and pepper.
2. Sear the Lamb:
    - In a large, heavy-bottomed pot or tagine, heat the olive oil over medium-high heat.
    - Add the lamb cubes in batches and sear them until browned on all sides. Remove the lamb and set aside.
3. Cook the Aromatics:
    - In the same pot or tagine, add the chopped onion and cook until softened, about 5 minutes.
    - Add the minced garlic, ground cumin, ground coriander, ground cinnamon, ground ginger, ground turmeric, and saffron threads (if using). Cook for another 1-2 minutes until fragrant.
4. Simmer the Tagine:
    - Stir in the tomato paste and cook for 1 minute.
    - Return the seared lamb cubes to the pot.

- Pour in the chicken broth or water and canned diced tomatoes with their juices. Stir well to combine.
5. Add Vegetables and Fruits:
    - Add the sliced carrots, diced potatoes, dried apricots, and golden raisins to the pot.
    - Stir in the lemon zest.
    - Bring the mixture to a boil, then reduce the heat to low. Cover the pot or tagine and let it simmer gently for 1.5 to 2 hours, or until the lamb is tender and the vegetables are cooked through.
6. Finish and Serve:
    - Taste and adjust seasoning with salt and pepper if needed.
    - Serve the Moroccan Lamb Tagine hot, garnished with chopped fresh cilantro or parsley.
    - Serve with cooked couscous or rice on the side.

Enjoy the rich flavors of this Moroccan Lamb Tagine, perfect for a cozy dinner for two!

Crab Cakes

Ingredients:

- 8 oz lump crab meat, drained and picked over for shells
- 1/4 cup breadcrumbs
- 1/4 cup mayonnaise
- 1 egg, lightly beaten
- 1 tablespoon Dijon mustard
- 1 tablespoon Worcestershire sauce
- 1 tablespoon lemon juice
- 1/4 teaspoon Old Bay seasoning (optional)
- Salt and pepper, to taste
- 2 tablespoons chopped fresh parsley
- 1/4 cup finely chopped green onions (green parts only)
- 2 tablespoons unsalted butter
- 2 tablespoons olive oil
- Lemon wedges, for serving
- Tartar sauce or remoulade sauce, for serving (optional)

Instructions:

1. Prepare the Crab Cakes Mixture:
    - In a large mixing bowl, combine the lump crab meat, breadcrumbs, mayonnaise, beaten egg, Dijon mustard, Worcestershire sauce, lemon juice, Old Bay seasoning (if using), salt, pepper, chopped parsley, and chopped green onions. Gently fold together until well combined, being careful not to break up the crab meat too much.
2. Form the Crab Cakes:
    - Divide the crab mixture into 4 equal portions. Shape each portion into a round cake, about 3 inches in diameter and 1 inch thick. Place the formed crab cakes on a plate or baking sheet lined with parchment paper.
3. Chill the Crab Cakes:
    - Refrigerate the crab cakes for at least 30 minutes to allow them to firm up. This step helps the crab cakes hold their shape better during cooking.
4. Cook the Crab Cakes:
    - In a large skillet, heat the butter and olive oil over medium-high heat until the butter is melted and sizzling.
    - Carefully place the crab cakes into the skillet, leaving space between each cake.
    - Cook the crab cakes for about 3-4 minutes on each side, or until they are golden brown and heated through. Use a spatula to carefully flip the crab cakes halfway through cooking.
5. Serve:
    - Remove the crab cakes from the skillet and drain on paper towels briefly to absorb any excess oil.

- - Serve the crab cakes hot, with lemon wedges on the side for squeezing over them.
  - Optionally, serve with tartar sauce or remoulade sauce on the side for dipping.

Enjoy your delicious Crab Cakes for Two, packed with crab meat and flavorful seasonings!

Sole Meunière

Ingredients:

- 2 sole fillets (about 6-8 ounces each), skinless
- Salt and pepper, to taste
- All-purpose flour, for dredging
- 3 tablespoons unsalted butter
- 1 tablespoon olive oil
- 2 tablespoons freshly squeezed lemon juice
- 2 tablespoons chopped fresh parsley
- Lemon wedges, for serving

Instructions:

1. Prepare the Sole:
    - Pat the sole fillets dry with paper towels.
    - Season both sides of the sole fillets with salt and pepper.
2. Dredge the Sole:
    - Dredge each sole fillet in flour, shaking off any excess.
3. Cook the Sole:
    - In a large skillet, heat 2 tablespoons of butter and the olive oil over medium-high heat.
    - Once the butter has melted and the skillet is hot, add the sole fillets to the skillet. Cook for about 2-3 minutes on each side, or until the fish is golden brown and cooked through. The flesh should be opaque and flake easily with a fork.
4. Make the Meunière Sauce:
    - Remove the cooked sole fillets from the skillet and transfer them to a serving plate. Cover loosely with foil to keep warm.
    - Add the remaining tablespoon of butter to the skillet. Cook over medium heat until the butter foams and turns a light brown color, about 1-2 minutes.
    - Remove the skillet from heat and carefully add the lemon juice to the browned butter, stirring gently to combine. Be cautious as the mixture may sizzle.
5. Serve:
    - Pour the meunière sauce over the cooked sole fillets.
    - Sprinkle with chopped fresh parsley.
    - Serve the Sole Meunière hot, with lemon wedges on the side for squeezing over the fish.

Enjoy your classic and flavorful Sole Meunière for Two!

Stuffed Bell Peppers

Ingredients:

- 2 large bell peppers (any color), tops cut off and seeds removed
- 1/2 pound ground beef (or ground turkey)
- 1/2 cup cooked rice (white or brown)
- 1/2 cup grated cheese (such as cheddar or mozzarella), divided
- 1/4 cup onion, finely chopped
- 1/4 cup tomato sauce or marinara sauce
- 1 clove garlic, minced
- 1/2 teaspoon dried oregano
- Salt and pepper, to taste
- Fresh parsley or basil, chopped, for garnish

Instructions:

1. Prepare the Bell Peppers:
    - Preheat your oven to 375°F (190°C).
    - Cut the tops off the bell peppers and remove the seeds and membranes. Set aside.
2. Prepare the Filling:
    - In a skillet, cook the ground beef (or turkey) over medium-high heat until browned and cooked through. Drain any excess fat.
    - Add the chopped onion and minced garlic to the skillet. Cook for 2-3 minutes until the onion is softened.
    - Stir in the cooked rice, half of the grated cheese, tomato sauce (or marinara sauce), dried oregano, salt, and pepper. Mix well until combined and heated through.
3. Stuff the Bell Peppers:
    - Place the hollowed-out bell peppers in a baking dish.
    - Spoon the filling mixture into each bell pepper, packing it tightly and mounding it on top.
    - Sprinkle the remaining grated cheese evenly over the tops of the stuffed bell peppers.
4. Bake:
    - Cover the baking dish with aluminum foil and bake in the preheated oven for 30-35 minutes, or until the bell peppers are tender and the filling is hot and bubbly.
5. Serve:
    - Remove the stuffed bell peppers from the oven.
    - Garnish with chopped fresh parsley or basil.
    - Serve hot, optionally with additional tomato sauce or marinara sauce on the side.

Enjoy your delicious Stuffed Bell Peppers for Two as a satisfying and flavorful meal!

Grilled Tuna Steak

Ingredients:

- 2 tuna steaks, about 6-8 ounces each, about 1 inch thick
- 2 tablespoons olive oil
- 2 cloves garlic, minced
- 1 teaspoon lemon zest
- 2 tablespoons lemon juice
- 1 tablespoon soy sauce
- 1 tablespoon honey
- Salt and pepper, to taste
- Fresh herbs (such as parsley or cilantro), chopped, for garnish
- Lemon wedges, for serving

Instructions:

1. Marinate the Tuna Steaks:
   - In a shallow dish or bowl, whisk together the olive oil, minced garlic, lemon zest, lemon juice, soy sauce, honey, salt, and pepper.
   - Place the tuna steaks in the marinade, turning to coat both sides. Let them marinate for at least 15-30 minutes at room temperature, or refrigerate for up to 2 hours.
2. Preheat the Grill:
   - Preheat your grill to medium-high heat. Make sure the grill grates are clean and lightly oiled to prevent sticking.
3. Grill the Tuna Steaks:
   - Remove the tuna steaks from the marinade and discard the marinade.
   - Place the tuna steaks on the preheated grill. Grill for 2-3 minutes per side for rare to medium-rare doneness, depending on the thickness of the steaks. For well-done, grill for 4-5 minutes per side.
4. Serve:
   - Remove the grilled tuna steaks from the grill and transfer them to a serving plate.
   - Sprinkle with chopped fresh herbs, such as parsley or cilantro.
   - Serve hot, with lemon wedges on the side for squeezing over the tuna steaks.

Enjoy your flavorful Grilled Tuna Steaks for Two, perfect for a light and satisfying meal!

Lemon Herb Roast Chicken

Ingredients:

- 1 whole chicken (about 3-4 pounds)
- Salt and pepper, to taste
- 2 tablespoons olive oil
- 1 lemon, halved
- 4 cloves garlic, minced
- 2 tablespoons chopped fresh herbs (such as rosemary, thyme, and parsley)
- 1 teaspoon paprika
- 1 teaspoon dried oregano
- 1/2 teaspoon dried basil
- 1/2 teaspoon dried thyme
- 1/2 teaspoon onion powder
- 1/2 teaspoon garlic powder
- 1/2 cup chicken broth or water
- Fresh herbs (such as parsley or thyme), for garnish (optional)

Instructions:

1. Preheat the Oven:
   - Preheat your oven to 400°F (200°C).
2. Prepare the Chicken:
   - Remove any giblets from the chicken cavity and pat the chicken dry with paper towels.
   - Season the chicken inside and out with salt and pepper.
3. Prepare the Herb Mixture:
   - In a small bowl, combine the olive oil, juice of half a lemon, minced garlic, chopped fresh herbs, paprika, dried oregano, dried basil, dried thyme, onion powder, and garlic powder. Mix well to form a paste.
4. Rub the Chicken:
   - Rub the herb mixture all over the chicken, including under the skin and inside the cavity. Ensure the chicken is evenly coated with the herb mixture.
5. Roast the Chicken:
   - Place the remaining lemon halves inside the chicken cavity.
   - Tie the legs together with kitchen twine, if desired, to help the chicken cook evenly.
   - Place the chicken breast side up on a roasting pan or baking dish.
   - Pour the chicken broth or water into the bottom of the pan.
6. Roast in the Oven:
   - Roast the chicken in the preheated oven for about 1 hour to 1 hour 15 minutes, or until the internal temperature reaches 165°F (74°C) when measured with a meat thermometer inserted into the thickest part of the thigh without touching bone.

7. Rest and Serve:
    - Once cooked, remove the chicken from the oven and let it rest for 10-15 minutes before carving.
    - Garnish with fresh herbs, if desired.
    - Serve the Lemon Herb Roast Chicken hot, accompanied by your favorite sides like roasted vegetables or potatoes.

Enjoy your delicious and flavorful Lemon Herb Roast Chicken for Two!

Shrimp and Grits

Ingredients:

- 1/2 cup stone-ground grits
- 2 cups chicken broth or water
- Salt and pepper, to taste
- 1/2 cup shredded cheddar cheese
- 1/2 pound shrimp, peeled and deveined
- 2 tablespoons unsalted butter
- 2 cloves garlic, minced
- 1/4 cup chopped green onions (green parts only)
- 1/4 cup cooked and crumbled bacon (optional)
- 1/2 cup heavy cream
- 1 tablespoon lemon juice
- 1/4 teaspoon Old Bay seasoning (optional)
- Fresh parsley, chopped, for garnish

Instructions:

1. Cook the Grits:
    - In a medium saucepan, bring the chicken broth (or water) to a boil.
    - Stir in the stone-ground grits and reduce the heat to low.
    - Cook the grits according to the package instructions, stirring occasionally, until they are creamy and tender, about 20-25 minutes.
    - Stir in the shredded cheddar cheese until melted and well combined. Season with salt and pepper to taste. Keep warm.
2. Prepare the Shrimp:
    - While the grits are cooking, season the shrimp with salt and pepper.
    - In a large skillet, melt 1 tablespoon of butter over medium-high heat.
    - Add the shrimp to the skillet and cook for 2-3 minutes per side, or until they are pink and cooked through. Remove the shrimp from the skillet and set aside.
3. Make the Sauce:
    - In the same skillet, melt the remaining 1 tablespoon of butter over medium heat.
    - Add the minced garlic and chopped green onions to the skillet. Cook for 1-2 minutes until fragrant.
    - If using, stir in the cooked and crumbled bacon.
4. Finish the Dish:
    - Pour in the heavy cream and lemon juice. Stir well to combine.
    - Season the sauce with Old Bay seasoning (if using), salt, and pepper to taste.
    - Add the cooked shrimp back to the skillet. Cook for another minute or two, stirring gently, until the shrimp are heated through and coated with the sauce.
5. Serve:
    - Divide the cheesy grits between two serving bowls.
    - Spoon the shrimp and sauce over the grits.

- Garnish with chopped fresh parsley.
  - Serve the Shrimp and Grits hot, optionally with additional hot sauce on the side.

Enjoy your comforting and flavorful Shrimp and Grits for Two!

Mushroom Risotto

Ingredients:

- 1/2 cup stone-ground grits
- 2 cups chicken broth or water
- Salt and pepper, to taste
- 1/2 cup shredded cheddar cheese
- 1/2 pound shrimp, peeled and deveined
- 2 tablespoons unsalted butter
- 2 cloves garlic, minced
- 1/4 cup chopped green onions (green parts only)
- 1/4 cup cooked and crumbled bacon (optional)
- 1/2 cup heavy cream
- 1 tablespoon lemon juice
- 1/4 teaspoon Old Bay seasoning (optional)
- Fresh parsley, chopped, for garnish

Instructions:

1. Cook the Grits:
    - In a medium saucepan, bring the chicken broth (or water) to a boil.
    - Stir in the stone-ground grits and reduce the heat to low.
    - Cook the grits according to the package instructions, stirring occasionally, until they are creamy and tender, about 20-25 minutes.
    - Stir in the shredded cheddar cheese until melted and well combined. Season with salt and pepper to taste. Keep warm.
2. Prepare the Shrimp:
    - While the grits are cooking, season the shrimp with salt and pepper.
    - In a large skillet, melt 1 tablespoon of butter over medium-high heat.
    - Add the shrimp to the skillet and cook for 2-3 minutes per side, or until they are pink and cooked through. Remove the shrimp from the skillet and set aside.
3. Make the Sauce:
    - In the same skillet, melt the remaining 1 tablespoon of butter over medium heat.
    - Add the minced garlic and chopped green onions to the skillet. Cook for 1-2 minutes until fragrant.
    - If using, stir in the cooked and crumbled bacon.
4. Finish the Dish:
    - Pour in the heavy cream and lemon juice. Stir well to combine.
    - Season the sauce with Old Bay seasoning (if using), salt, and pepper to taste.
    - Add the cooked shrimp back to the skillet. Cook for another minute or two, stirring gently, until the shrimp are heated through and coated with the sauce.
5. Serve:
    - Divide the cheesy grits between two serving bowls.
    - Spoon the shrimp and sauce over the grits.

- Garnish with chopped fresh parsley.
- Serve the Shrimp and Grits hot, optionally with additional hot sauce on the side.

Enjoy your comforting and flavorful Shrimp and Grits for Two!

Mushroom Risotto

Ingredients:

- 1 cup Arborio rice
- 4 cups chicken or vegetable broth
- 1/2 cup dry white wine
- 2 tablespoons unsalted butter, divided
- 1 tablespoon olive oil
- 1/2 cup finely chopped onion
- 2 cloves garlic, minced
- 8 oz mushrooms (such as cremini or shiitake), sliced
- 1/2 cup grated Parmesan cheese
- Salt and pepper, to taste
- Fresh parsley, chopped, for garnish

Instructions:

1. Prepare the Broth:
    - In a saucepan, heat the chicken or vegetable broth over medium heat. Keep it warm throughout the cooking process.
2. Cook the Mushrooms:
    - In a large skillet or sauté pan, heat 1 tablespoon of butter and 1 tablespoon of olive oil over medium-high heat.
    - Add the sliced mushrooms and cook for 5-7 minutes, stirring occasionally, until they are browned and tender. Season with salt and pepper. Remove the mushrooms from the skillet and set aside.
3. Prepare the Risotto:
    - In the same skillet, melt the remaining tablespoon of butter over medium heat.
    - Add the chopped onion and cook for 3-4 minutes until softened.
    - Add the minced garlic and cook for another 1 minute until fragrant.
4. Toast the Rice:
    - Add the Arborio rice to the skillet with the onions and garlic. Stir well to coat the rice with the butter and cook for 1-2 minutes until the rice becomes translucent around the edges.
5. Deglaze with Wine:
    - Pour in the dry white wine and stir constantly until the wine is absorbed by the rice.
6. Add the Broth:
    - Begin adding the warm broth to the rice mixture, one ladleful (about 1/2 cup) at a time.
    - Stir constantly and allow each addition of broth to be absorbed by the rice before adding the next ladleful.
    - Continue this process for about 18-20 minutes, or until the rice is creamy and cooked al dente. You may not need to use all of the broth.

7. Finish the Risotto:
    - Stir in the cooked mushrooms and grated Parmesan cheese.
    - Season with salt and pepper to taste. The risotto should be creamy and slightly runny (all'onda).
8. Serve:
    - Remove the mushroom risotto from heat and let it rest for a minute or two.
    - Garnish with chopped fresh parsley.
    - Serve hot as a main dish or alongside grilled meats or seafood.

Enjoy your creamy and flavorful Mushroom Risotto for Two!

Spaghetti Carbonara

Ingredients:

- 6 oz spaghetti
- 2 large eggs
- 1/2 cup grated Pecorino Romano cheese (or Parmesan), plus extra for serving
- 4 slices of pancetta or bacon, diced
- 2 cloves garlic, minced
- 1 tablespoon unsalted butter
- Salt and black pepper, to taste
- Fresh parsley, chopped, for garnish

Instructions:

1. Cook the Pasta:
    - Cook the spaghetti in a large pot of boiling salted water according to the package instructions until al dente. Reserve about 1/2 cup of pasta water before draining.
2. Prepare the Sauce:
    - While the pasta is cooking, in a bowl, whisk together the eggs and grated Pecorino Romano cheese. Season with black pepper.
3. Cook the Pancetta (or Bacon):
    - In a large skillet, cook the diced pancetta (or bacon) over medium heat until crisp. Remove from the skillet and drain on paper towels.
4. Make the Carbonara Sauce:
    - In the same skillet, discard excess fat, leaving about 1 tablespoon. Add the minced garlic and cook for about 1 minute until fragrant.
    - Add the cooked pancetta (or bacon) back to the skillet along with the butter. Stir to combine and heat through.
5. Combine Pasta and Sauce:
    - Add the cooked and drained spaghetti to the skillet with the pancetta (or bacon) and toss to coat evenly with the garlic and pancetta mixture.
6. Add the Egg Mixture:
    - Remove the skillet from heat. Quickly pour the egg and cheese mixture over the pasta, tossing quickly and continuously to coat the pasta evenly. The heat from the pasta will cook the eggs and create a creamy sauce. If needed, add some of the reserved pasta water to loosen the sauce.
7. Serve:
    - Divide the spaghetti carbonara between two serving plates.
    - Garnish with extra grated Pecorino Romano cheese, black pepper, and chopped fresh parsley.

Enjoy your delicious and creamy Spaghetti Carbonara for Two!

Chicken Alfredo

Ingredients:

- 6 oz fettuccine pasta
- 2 boneless, skinless chicken breasts, thinly sliced
- Salt and pepper, to taste
- 2 tablespoons olive oil
- 2 tablespoons unsalted butter
- 2 cloves garlic, minced
- 1 cup heavy cream
- 1 cup grated Parmesan cheese, plus extra for serving
- 1/2 teaspoon garlic powder
- 1/2 teaspoon onion powder
- 1/4 teaspoon nutmeg (optional)
- Fresh parsley, chopped, for garnish

Instructions:

1. Cook the Pasta:
    - Cook the fettuccine pasta in a large pot of boiling salted water according to the package instructions until al dente. Reserve about 1/2 cup of pasta water before draining.
2. Prepare the Chicken:
    - Season the thinly sliced chicken breasts with salt and pepper.
    - In a large skillet, heat the olive oil over medium-high heat. Add the chicken slices and cook for 3-4 minutes per side, or until cooked through and golden brown. Remove the chicken from the skillet and set aside.
3. Make the Alfredo Sauce:
    - In the same skillet, melt the butter over medium heat.
    - Add the minced garlic and cook for about 1 minute until fragrant.
    - Pour in the heavy cream, stirring constantly. Bring the cream to a simmer.
4. Add Cheese and Seasonings:
    - Gradually stir in the grated Parmesan cheese, garlic powder, onion powder, and nutmeg (if using). Continue stirring until the cheese is melted and the sauce is smooth and creamy. Season with salt and pepper to taste.
5. Combine Pasta, Chicken, and Sauce:
    - Add the cooked fettuccine pasta to the skillet with the Alfredo sauce. Toss to coat the pasta evenly in the sauce.
    - Add the cooked chicken slices back to the skillet, stirring gently to combine with the pasta and sauce. If needed, add some of the reserved pasta water to adjust the consistency of the sauce.
6. Serve:
    - Divide the Chicken Alfredo between two serving plates.
    - Garnish with extra grated Parmesan cheese and chopped fresh parsley.

- Serve hot, optionally with a side of garlic bread or a green salad.

Enjoy your creamy and indulgent Chicken Alfredo for Two!

Veal Marsala

Ingredients:

- 2 veal scallopini (about 1/2 pound total), pounded thin
- Salt and pepper, to taste
- 1/4 cup all-purpose flour, for dredging
- 2 tablespoons unsalted butter
- 1 tablespoon olive oil
- 1/2 cup sliced mushrooms
- 1/4 cup Marsala wine
- 1/4 cup chicken broth
- 1/4 cup heavy cream
- Fresh parsley, chopped, for garnish

Instructions:

1. Prepare the Veal:
    - Season the veal scallopini with salt and pepper on both sides.
    - Dredge the veal in flour, shaking off any excess.
2. Cook the Veal:
    - In a large skillet, heat 1 tablespoon of butter and 1 tablespoon of olive oil over medium-high heat.
    - Add the veal scallopini to the skillet and cook for about 2-3 minutes on each side, or until golden brown and cooked through. Remove the veal from the skillet and set aside.
3. Make the Marsala Sauce:
    - In the same skillet, add the remaining tablespoon of butter.
    - Add the sliced mushrooms to the skillet and cook for about 3-4 minutes, or until they are softened and lightly browned.
4. Deglaze and Simmer:
    - Pour in the Marsala wine and chicken broth, stirring to scrape up any browned bits from the bottom of the skillet.
    - Allow the sauce to come to a simmer and cook for 2-3 minutes, or until slightly reduced.
5. Finish the Sauce:
    - Stir in the heavy cream and continue cooking for another 1-2 minutes until the sauce thickens slightly.
6. Serve:
    - Return the cooked veal scallopini to the skillet, spooning some of the Marsala sauce over the top.
    - Garnish with chopped fresh parsley.
    - Serve the Veal Marsala hot, accompanied by pasta or mashed potatoes, if desired.

Enjoy your delicious and savory Veal Marsala for Two, rich with flavors from Marsala wine and mushrooms!

Baked Ziti

Ingredients:

- 6 oz ziti pasta (or penne)
- 1/2 pound ground Italian sausage or ground beef
- 1/2 cup diced onion
- 2 cloves garlic, minced
- 1 cup marinara sauce
- 1/2 cup ricotta cheese
- 1 cup shredded mozzarella cheese, divided
- 1/4 cup grated Parmesan cheese
- 1/2 teaspoon dried oregano
- 1/2 teaspoon dried basil
- Salt and pepper, to taste
- Fresh basil or parsley, chopped, for garnish

Instructions:

1. Preheat Oven:
   - Preheat your oven to 375°F (190°C). Lightly grease a baking dish (about 8x8 inches or similar size) with olive oil or non-stick spray.
2. Cook the Pasta:
   - Cook the ziti pasta according to package instructions until al dente. Drain and set aside.
3. Prepare the Meat Sauce:
   - In a large skillet, cook the ground Italian sausage (or ground beef) over medium-high heat until browned and cooked through, breaking it up with a spoon as it cooks.
   - Add the diced onion and minced garlic to the skillet. Cook for 3-4 minutes until the onion is softened and translucent.
4. Combine Sauce and Pasta:
   - Stir in the marinara sauce, dried oregano, and dried basil. Season with salt and pepper to taste. Simmer for a few minutes to blend the flavors.
   - Add the cooked ziti pasta to the skillet with the meat sauce. Stir to coat the pasta evenly.
5. Assemble the Baked Ziti:
   - In a small bowl, mix together the ricotta cheese and half of the shredded mozzarella cheese.
   - Spread half of the pasta mixture evenly into the prepared baking dish.
   - Dollop spoonfuls of the ricotta cheese mixture over the pasta.
   - Sprinkle with the remaining shredded mozzarella cheese and grated Parmesan cheese.
6. Bake the Ziti:

- Cover the baking dish with aluminum foil and bake in the preheated oven for 20 minutes.
- Remove the foil and bake for an additional 10 minutes, or until the cheese is melted and bubbly.

7. Serve:
    - Remove the baked ziti from the oven and let it rest for a few minutes.
    - Garnish with chopped fresh basil or parsley.
    - Serve the Baked Ziti hot, optionally with a side salad and garlic bread.

Enjoy your hearty and comforting Baked Ziti for Two, perfect for a cozy meal at home!

Grilled Swordfish

Ingredients:

- 2 swordfish steaks, about 6-8 ounces each
- Salt and pepper, to taste
- 2 tablespoons olive oil
- 1 tablespoon lemon juice
- 2 cloves garlic, minced
- 1 teaspoon dried oregano
- 1/2 teaspoon paprika
- Lemon wedges, for serving
- Fresh parsley, chopped, for garnish

Instructions:

1. Prepare the Swordfish Steaks:
    - Pat the swordfish steaks dry with paper towels.
    - Season both sides of the steaks generously with salt and pepper.
2. Make the Marinade:
    - In a small bowl, whisk together the olive oil, lemon juice, minced garlic, dried oregano, and paprika.
3. Marinate the Swordfish:
    - Place the swordfish steaks in a shallow dish or resealable plastic bag.
    - Pour the marinade over the swordfish steaks, turning to coat evenly. Allow them to marinate in the refrigerator for at least 30 minutes, or up to 2 hours.
4. Preheat the Grill:
    - Preheat your grill to medium-high heat. Make sure the grill grates are clean and lightly oiled.
5. Grill the Swordfish:
    - Remove the swordfish steaks from the marinade, shaking off any excess.
    - Place the swordfish steaks on the preheated grill. Grill for about 4-5 minutes per side, depending on the thickness of the steaks, or until the fish is cooked through and easily flakes with a fork. Avoid overcooking to keep the swordfish moist and tender.
6. Serve:
    - Remove the grilled swordfish steaks from the grill and transfer them to a serving platter.
    - Garnish with chopped fresh parsley and serve hot, with lemon wedges on the side for squeezing over the fish.

Enjoy your delicious Grilled Swordfish for Two, a perfect dish for a special dinner!

Duck Breast with Raspberry Sauce

Ingredients:

- 2 duck breasts
- Salt and pepper, to taste
- 1 tablespoon olive oil
- 1 shallot, finely chopped
- 1/2 cup dry red wine (such as Merlot or Cabernet Sauvignon)
- 1/2 cup chicken or beef broth
- 1/4 cup raspberry preserves or fresh raspberries
- 1 tablespoon balsamic vinegar
- 1 tablespoon unsalted butter
- Fresh thyme sprigs, for garnish

Instructions:

1. Prepare the Duck Breasts:
    - Score the skin of the duck breasts in a crosshatch pattern with a sharp knife, being careful not to cut into the meat.
    - Season both sides of the duck breasts generously with salt and pepper.
2. Sear the Duck Breasts:
    - Heat a large skillet over medium-high heat. Place the duck breasts skin-side down in the skillet, without adding any oil. Sear for about 6-8 minutes, or until the skin is crispy and golden brown. Flip the duck breasts and cook for another 4-6 minutes for medium-rare, or longer to desired doneness. Transfer the duck breasts to a plate and let them rest, loosely covered with foil.
3. Make the Raspberry Sauce:
    - In the same skillet, reduce the heat to medium. Add the finely chopped shallot and cook for 2-3 minutes until softened.
    - Pour in the dry red wine and chicken or beef broth, stirring to scrape up any browned bits from the bottom of the skillet. Simmer for about 5 minutes until the liquid is reduced by half.
4. Finish the Sauce:
    - Stir in the raspberry preserves (or fresh raspberries) and balsamic vinegar. Simmer for another 3-4 minutes until the sauce has thickened slightly.
5. Add Butter and Serve:
    - Remove the skillet from heat and swirl in the unsalted butter until melted and incorporated into the sauce. Season with salt and pepper to taste.
6. Slice and Serve:
    - Slice the duck breasts diagonally into thin slices.
    - Arrange the sliced duck breasts on serving plates and drizzle with the raspberry sauce.
    - Garnish with fresh thyme sprigs.
7. Serve Hot:

- Serve the Duck Breast with Raspberry Sauce immediately, accompanied by your choice of side dishes like roasted vegetables or mashed potatoes.

Enjoy your elegant and flavorful Duck Breast with Raspberry Sauce for Two, perfect for a special occasion dinner!

Stuffed Portobello Mushrooms

Ingredients:

- 2 large Portobello mushrooms
- 1 tablespoon olive oil
- 2 cloves garlic, minced
- 1/2 cup diced onion
- 1/2 cup diced bell pepper (any color)
- 1/2 cup diced zucchini
- 1/2 cup diced tomato
- 1/2 cup fresh spinach, chopped
- 1/2 cup breadcrumbs
- 1/4 cup grated Parmesan cheese
- 1/4 cup shredded mozzarella cheese
- 1 tablespoon chopped fresh parsley
- Salt and pepper, to taste
- Pinch of red pepper flakes (optional)
- Balsamic glaze, for drizzling (optional)
- Fresh basil leaves, for garnish

Instructions:

1. Prepare the Portobello Mushrooms:
   - Preheat your oven to 375°F (190°C). Line a baking sheet with parchment paper.
   - Clean the Portobello mushrooms and gently remove the stems. Use a spoon to scrape out the gills from the underside of the mushrooms to create more space for the stuffing.
2. Prepare the Stuffing:
   - In a large skillet, heat the olive oil over medium heat. Add the minced garlic and diced onion. Cook for 2-3 minutes until the onion starts to soften.
3. Add Vegetables:
   - Add the diced bell pepper, zucchini, and tomato to the skillet. Cook for another 5-7 minutes until the vegetables are tender.
4. Combine Ingredients:
   - Stir in the chopped spinach and cook for 1-2 minutes until wilted. Remove the skillet from heat.
5. Mix with Breadcrumbs and Cheese:
   - In a bowl, combine the cooked vegetables with breadcrumbs, grated Parmesan cheese, shredded mozzarella cheese, chopped fresh parsley, salt, pepper, and red pepper flakes (if using). Mix well until everything is evenly combined.
6. Stuff the Mushrooms:
   - Place the Portobello mushrooms on the prepared baking sheet, gill-side up.
   - Spoon the vegetable mixture evenly into each mushroom cap, pressing down gently to pack it in.

7. Bake:
    - Bake in the preheated oven for 20-25 minutes, or until the mushrooms are tender and the stuffing is golden brown and crispy on top.
8. Serve:
    - Remove the stuffed Portobello mushrooms from the oven.
    - Drizzle with balsamic glaze, if desired, and garnish with fresh basil leaves.

Enjoy your delicious Stuffed Portobello Mushrooms for Two as a flavorful and satisfying vegetarian meal!

Pan-Seared Sea Bass

Ingredients:

- 2 sea bass fillets, about 6-8 ounces each, skin-on
- Salt and pepper, to taste
- 2 tablespoons olive oil
- 2 cloves garlic, minced
- 1 tablespoon unsalted butter
- 1 lemon, cut into wedges
- Fresh parsley, chopped, for garnish

Instructions:

1. Prepare the Sea Bass:
   - Pat the sea bass fillets dry with paper towels. Season both sides generously with salt and pepper.
2. Heat the Pan:
   - In a large skillet, heat the olive oil over medium-high heat until shimmering.
3. Sear the Sea Bass:
   - Place the sea bass fillets in the skillet, skin-side down. Cook for about 4-5 minutes without moving them, or until the skin is crispy and golden brown. Press down gently with a spatula to ensure even cooking.
4. Flip and Cook:
   - Carefully flip the sea bass fillets using a spatula. Cook for another 3-4 minutes, or until the flesh is opaque and flakes easily with a fork. Adjust cooking time based on the thickness of the fillets.
5. Add Garlic and Butter:
   - Add the minced garlic and unsalted butter to the skillet. Tilt the skillet slightly and spoon the melted butter over the sea bass fillets continuously for about 1 minute, to infuse the fish with flavor.
6. Serve:
   - Remove the sea bass fillets from the skillet and transfer them to serving plates.
   - Squeeze fresh lemon juice over the fillets.
   - Garnish with chopped fresh parsley.
7. Serve Hot:
   - Serve the Pan-Seared Sea Bass immediately, accompanied by your favorite sides such as steamed vegetables, rice, or a fresh salad.

Enjoy your delicious and tender Pan-Seared Sea Bass for Two, showcasing the delicate flavors of the fish with a crispy skin finish!

Tortellini Alfredo

Ingredients:

- 8 oz cheese tortellini (fresh or frozen)
- 1/4 cup unsalted butter
- 1 cup heavy cream
- 1 cup grated Parmesan cheese, plus extra for serving
- Salt and pepper, to taste
- Fresh parsley, chopped, for garnish

Instructions:

1. Cook the Tortellini:
    - Cook the cheese tortellini in a large pot of boiling salted water according to the package instructions until al dente. Drain and set aside.
2. Make the Alfredo Sauce:
    - In a large skillet or saucepan, melt the unsalted butter over medium heat.
    - Pour in the heavy cream and bring to a simmer. Cook for about 5 minutes, stirring occasionally, until the cream starts to thicken slightly.
3. Add Parmesan Cheese:
    - Gradually stir in the grated Parmesan cheese, a little at a time, until the cheese is melted and the sauce is smooth and creamy. Season with salt and pepper to taste.
4. Combine Tortellini and Sauce:
    - Add the cooked tortellini to the skillet with the Alfredo sauce. Toss gently to coat the tortellini evenly with the sauce.
5. Serve:
    - Divide the Tortellini Alfredo between two serving plates.
    - Garnish with extra grated Parmesan cheese and chopped fresh parsley.
6. Enjoy:
    - Serve the Tortellini Alfredo hot, optionally with a side of garlic bread or a crisp green salad.

This Tortellini Alfredo for Two is creamy, comforting, and perfect for a cozy dinner at home!

Steak Diane

Ingredients:

- 2 beef tenderloin steaks, about 6-8 ounces each
- Salt and pepper, to taste
- 1 tablespoon olive oil
- 2 tablespoons unsalted butter, divided
- 2 cloves garlic, minced
- 1/4 cup finely chopped shallots or onion
- 1/4 cup brandy or cognac
- 1/2 cup beef broth
- 1/4 cup heavy cream
- 1 tablespoon Dijon mustard
- 1 tablespoon Worcestershire sauce
- 2 tablespoons chopped fresh parsley, for garnish
- Lemon wedges, for serving

Instructions:

1. Prepare the Steaks:
    - Season both sides of the beef tenderloin steaks generously with salt and pepper.
2. Sear the Steaks:
    - In a large skillet, heat the olive oil over medium-high heat until hot but not smoking.
    - Add the steaks to the skillet and cook for about 3-4 minutes per side for medium-rare, or longer to your desired doneness. Remove the steaks from the skillet and set aside on a plate, loosely covered with foil to keep warm.
3. Make the Sauce:
    - Reduce the heat to medium and add 1 tablespoon of butter to the skillet.
    - Add the minced garlic and finely chopped shallots (or onion) to the skillet. Cook for about 2-3 minutes until softened.
4. Flambé with Brandy:
    - Carefully pour the brandy or cognac into the skillet. Using a long match or lighter, ignite the alcohol to flambé. Allow the flames to burn off naturally or carefully extinguish them by covering the skillet with a lid.
5. Add Broth and Cream:
    - Once the flames subside, stir in the beef broth and bring to a simmer. Cook for about 2-3 minutes, stirring occasionally, until the sauce reduces slightly.
6. Finish the Sauce:
    - Stir in the heavy cream, Dijon mustard, Worcestershire sauce, and remaining tablespoon of butter. Cook for another 2-3 minutes until the sauce thickens to your desired consistency.
7. Serve:

- Return the cooked steaks to the skillet, turning to coat them with the sauce. Heat for a minute or two to warm the steaks through.
- Transfer the steaks to serving plates. Spoon the sauce over the steaks and garnish with chopped fresh parsley.
8. Garnish and Serve:
    - Serve the Steak Diane hot, accompanied by lemon wedges on the side for squeezing over the steak.

Enjoy your elegant and flavorful Steak Diane for Two, a classic dish with a rich and creamy sauce!

Fettuccine Alfredo with Shrimp

Ingredients:

- 6 oz fettuccine pasta
- 10-12 large shrimp, peeled and deveined
- Salt and pepper, to taste
- 2 tablespoons unsalted butter
- 2 cloves garlic, minced
- 1 cup heavy cream
- 1 cup grated Parmesan cheese
- 1/2 teaspoon garlic powder
- 1/2 teaspoon onion powder
- Pinch of nutmeg (optional)
- Fresh parsley, chopped, for garnish

Instructions:

1. Cook the Pasta:
    - Cook the fettuccine pasta in a large pot of boiling salted water according to the package instructions until al dente. Drain and set aside.
2. Prepare the Shrimp:
    - Pat the shrimp dry with paper towels. Season with salt and pepper.
    - In a large skillet, melt 1 tablespoon of butter over medium-high heat. Add the minced garlic and cook for about 1 minute until fragrant.
    - Add the shrimp to the skillet and cook for 2-3 minutes per side, or until pink and cooked through. Remove the shrimp from the skillet and set aside.
3. Make the Alfredo Sauce:
    - In the same skillet, add the remaining tablespoon of butter. Pour in the heavy cream and bring to a simmer over medium heat.
    - Gradually stir in the grated Parmesan cheese, garlic powder, onion powder, and nutmeg (if using). Stir constantly until the cheese is melted and the sauce is smooth and creamy. Season with salt and pepper to taste.
4. Combine Pasta, Shrimp, and Sauce:
    - Add the cooked fettuccine pasta to the skillet with the Alfredo sauce. Toss to coat the pasta evenly in the sauce.
    - Add the cooked shrimp back to the skillet, stirring gently to combine with the pasta and sauce. Heat for another minute or two until everything is heated through.
5. Serve:
    - Divide the Fettuccine Alfredo with Shrimp between two serving plates.
    - Garnish with chopped fresh parsley.
6. Enjoy:
    - Serve hot, optionally with a sprinkle of extra Parmesan cheese and a side of garlic bread or a green salad.

This Fettuccine Alfredo with Shrimp for Two is creamy, indulgent, and perfect for a cozy dinner together!

Lamb Shank

Ingredients:

- 2 lamb shanks
- Salt and pepper, to taste
- 2 tablespoons olive oil
- 1 onion, chopped
- 2 carrots, chopped
- 2 celery stalks, chopped
- 4 cloves garlic, minced
- 1 cup red wine (such as Merlot or Cabernet Sauvignon)
- 2 cups beef or lamb broth
- 2 sprigs fresh rosemary
- 2 sprigs fresh thyme
- 2 bay leaves
- 1 tablespoon tomato paste
- 1 tablespoon Worcestershire sauce
- Mashed potatoes or polenta, for serving
- Chopped fresh parsley, for garnish

Instructions:

1. Preheat and Season:
    - Preheat your oven to 325°F (160°C).
    - Season the lamb shanks generously with salt and pepper.
2. Sear the Lamb Shanks:
    - In a large oven-safe Dutch oven or skillet, heat the olive oil over medium-high heat.
    - Add the lamb shanks and sear on all sides until browned, about 4-5 minutes per side. Remove the lamb shanks and set aside.
3. Prepare the Vegetables:
    - In the same Dutch oven or skillet, add the chopped onion, carrots, and celery. Cook for about 5 minutes, stirring occasionally, until softened.
4. Deglaze and Simmer:
    - Add the minced garlic and cook for another minute until fragrant.
    - Pour in the red wine, scraping up any browned bits from the bottom of the pan.
    - Stir in the beef or lamb broth, fresh rosemary, thyme sprigs, bay leaves, tomato paste, and Worcestershire sauce. Bring to a simmer.
5. Braise the Lamb Shanks:
    - Return the lamb shanks to the Dutch oven, nestling them into the liquid and vegetables.
    - Cover the Dutch oven with a lid and transfer it to the preheated oven.

- Braise for 2.5 to 3 hours, or until the lamb shanks are tender and falling off the bone. Check occasionally and add more broth if needed to keep the shanks partially submerged.

6. **Serve:**
    - Remove the lamb shanks from the Dutch oven and place them on serving plates.
    - Strain the braising liquid and vegetables through a fine mesh sieve, discarding the solids. Skim off any excess fat from the surface of the liquid.
    - Serve the lamb shanks over mashed potatoes or polenta, spooning the strained braising liquid over the top.
    - Garnish with chopped fresh parsley.
7. **Enjoy:**
    - Serve the Braised Lamb Shanks hot, with a side of your choice and enjoy the tender, flavorful meat.

This Braised Lamb Shank for Two is a comforting and hearty dish, perfect for a special meal together.

Herb-Crusted Salmon

Ingredients:

- 2 salmon fillets, skin-on, about 6-8 ounces each
- Salt and pepper, to taste
- 2 tablespoons Dijon mustard
- 1/4 cup panko breadcrumbs
- 2 tablespoons grated Parmesan cheese
- 1 tablespoon chopped fresh parsley
- 1 tablespoon chopped fresh dill (or 1 teaspoon dried dill)
- 1 tablespoon chopped fresh chives (or 1 teaspoon dried chives)
- 1 tablespoon olive oil
- Lemon wedges, for serving

Instructions:

1. Preheat Oven:
    - Preheat your oven to 400°F (200°C). Line a baking sheet with parchment paper or foil.
2. Prepare Salmon Fillets:
    - Pat the salmon fillets dry with paper towels. Season both sides with salt and pepper.
3. Coat with Dijon Mustard:
    - Brush the skin-side of the salmon fillets with Dijon mustard.
4. Prepare Herb Crust:
    - In a small bowl, combine panko breadcrumbs, grated Parmesan cheese, chopped fresh parsley, dill, and chives. Mix well.
5. Coat with Herb Crust:
    - Press the herb mixture onto the Dijon-coated side of each salmon fillet, ensuring an even coating.
6. Sear the Salmon:
    - In an oven-safe skillet, heat olive oil over medium-high heat. Place the salmon fillets herb-side down in the skillet and sear for 2-3 minutes, or until the crust is golden brown and crispy.
7. Bake the Salmon:
    - Transfer the skillet to the preheated oven and bake for 8-10 minutes, or until the salmon is cooked through and flakes easily with a fork.
8. Serve:
    - Remove the herb-crusted salmon from the oven and let it rest for a few minutes.
    - Serve the salmon fillets hot, with lemon wedges on the side for squeezing over the fish.

Enjoy your delicious Herb-Crusted Salmon for Two, with a crispy herb topping that adds wonderful flavor and texture to the tender salmon fillets!

Chicken Cordon Bleu

Ingredients:

- 2 boneless, skinless chicken breasts
- Salt and pepper, to taste
- 4 slices Swiss cheese
- 4 slices ham (thinly sliced)
- 1/2 cup all-purpose flour
- 1 egg, beaten
- 1 cup breadcrumbs (preferably panko breadcrumbs)
- 2 tablespoons grated Parmesan cheese
- 2 tablespoons unsalted butter
- 2 tablespoons olive oil
- Toothpicks or kitchen twine

Instructions:

1. Prepare the Chicken Breasts:
    - Preheat your oven to 375°F (190°C).
    - Place one chicken breast between two sheets of plastic wrap or parchment paper. Use a meat mallet or rolling pin to pound the chicken breast to an even thickness of about 1/4 inch. Repeat with the other chicken breast. Season both sides of each chicken breast with salt and pepper.
2. Assemble the Chicken Cordon Bleu:
    - Place two slices of Swiss cheese and two slices of ham on each chicken breast, folding them to fit if necessary. Roll up each chicken breast, starting from the short end, and secure with toothpicks or tie with kitchen twine to hold the shape.
3. Coat the Chicken:
    - Prepare three shallow bowls or plates: one with flour, one with beaten egg, and one with breadcrumbs mixed with grated Parmesan cheese.
    - Dredge each rolled chicken breast first in the flour, shaking off any excess. Dip into the beaten egg, allowing any excess to drip off. Finally, coat evenly with the breadcrumb mixture, pressing gently to adhere.
4. Cook the Chicken:
    - In a large oven-safe skillet, heat the butter and olive oil over medium-high heat until the butter is melted and foamy.
    - Carefully place the chicken breasts seam-side down in the skillet. Cook for about 3-4 minutes per side, or until golden brown and crispy.
5. Bake the Chicken:
    - Transfer the skillet to the preheated oven. Bake for 20-25 minutes, or until the chicken is cooked through (internal temperature should reach 165°F or 75°C) and the cheese is melted.
6. Serve:
    - Remove the chicken cordon bleu from the oven and let it rest for a few minutes.

- Remove the toothpicks or kitchen twine before serving.
- Optionally, slice each chicken breast diagonally and serve with a side of steamed vegetables or salad.

Enjoy your delicious homemade Chicken Cordon Bleu for Two, with crispy breadcrumb coating, melted cheese, and savory ham inside tender chicken breasts!

Grilled Ribeye Steak

Ingredients:

- 2 ribeye steaks, about 1 inch thick
- Salt and pepper, to taste
- 2 tablespoons olive oil
- 2 cloves garlic, minced (optional)
- Fresh herbs (such as rosemary and thyme), chopped (optional)
- Butter, for serving (optional)

Instructions:

1. Preheat the Grill:
    - Preheat your grill to high heat (about 450-500°F or 230-260°C).
2. Prepare the Steaks:
    - Remove the ribeye steaks from the refrigerator and let them come to room temperature, about 30 minutes.
    - Pat the steaks dry with paper towels and season both sides generously with salt and pepper.
3. Optional Marinade:
    - If desired, mix olive oil, minced garlic, and chopped fresh herbs in a small bowl. Rub this mixture onto both sides of the steaks.
4. Grill the Steaks:
    - Place the ribeye steaks on the hot grill grates. For a 1-inch thick steak, grill for about 4-5 minutes per side for medium-rare, or adjust the cooking time according to your preferred doneness:
        - Rare: 3-4 minutes per side
        - Medium: 5-6 minutes per side
        - Well-done: 7-8 minutes per side
5. Rest the Steaks:
    - Once cooked to your liking, remove the steaks from the grill and transfer them to a cutting board or plate. Tent loosely with foil and let them rest for 5-10 minutes. This allows the juices to redistribute within the meat.
6. Serve:
    - After resting, slice the ribeye steaks against the grain into thick slices.
    - Serve hot, optionally with a pat of butter on top.
7. Enjoy:
    - Serve the Grilled Ribeye Steak for Two with your favorite side dishes such as roasted vegetables, baked potatoes, or a fresh salad.

This Grilled Ribeye Steak recipe ensures tender, juicy steaks with a deliciously charred exterior, perfect for a special dinner for two! Adjust cooking times based on steak thickness and desired doneness for best results.

Shrimp Fra Diavolo

Ingredients:

- 10-12 large shrimp, peeled and deveined
- Salt and pepper, to taste
- 1 tablespoon olive oil
- 2 cloves garlic, minced
- 1/2 teaspoon red pepper flakes (adjust to taste)
- 1/2 cup dry white wine (such as Pinot Grigio or Sauvignon Blanc)
- 1 can (14.5 oz) diced tomatoes
- 1/2 teaspoon dried oregano
- 1/2 teaspoon dried basil
- 4 oz linguine or spaghetti pasta
- Fresh basil leaves, chopped, for garnish
- Grated Parmesan cheese, for serving (optional)

Instructions:

1. Prepare the Shrimp:
    - Pat the shrimp dry with paper towels. Season with salt and pepper.
2. Cook the Pasta:
    - Cook the linguine or spaghetti pasta in a large pot of salted boiling water according to package instructions until al dente. Drain and set aside.
3. Make the Sauce:
    - In a large skillet, heat olive oil over medium heat. Add minced garlic and red pepper flakes. Cook for about 1 minute until fragrant.
4. Deglaze with Wine:
    - Pour in the dry white wine and simmer for 2-3 minutes, allowing the alcohol to cook off and the liquid to reduce slightly.
5. Add Tomatoes and Herbs:
    - Stir in the diced tomatoes (with their juices), dried oregano, and dried basil. Bring to a simmer and cook for about 5-7 minutes, stirring occasionally, until the sauce thickens slightly.
6. Cook the Shrimp:
    - Add the seasoned shrimp to the skillet with the tomato sauce. Cook for 3-4 minutes, or until the shrimp are pink and cooked through. Avoid overcooking.
7. Combine Pasta and Sauce:
    - Add the cooked linguine or spaghetti pasta to the skillet with the shrimp and sauce. Toss gently to coat the pasta evenly with the sauce.
8. Serve:
    - Divide the Shrimp Fra Diavolo between two serving plates.
    - Garnish with chopped fresh basil leaves and grated Parmesan cheese, if desired.
9. Enjoy:
    - Serve immediately, with crusty bread on the side if desired.

This Shrimp Fra Diavolo for Two is spicy, flavorful, and perfect for a romantic dinner at home. Adjust the red pepper flakes to suit your spice preference.

Pork Chops with Sage Butter

Ingredients:

- 2 bone-in pork chops, about 1 inch thick
- Salt and pepper, to taste
- 2 tablespoons olive oil
- 2 tablespoons unsalted butter
- 4-6 fresh sage leaves
- 2 cloves garlic, minced
- 1/4 cup chicken broth or white wine
- 1 tablespoon Dijon mustard
- 1/4 cup heavy cream (optional)
- Fresh parsley, chopped, for garnish

Instructions:

1. Prepare the Pork Chops:
    - Pat the pork chops dry with paper towels. Season both sides generously with salt and pepper.
2. Sear the Pork Chops:
    - In a large skillet, heat olive oil over medium-high heat until shimmering.
    - Add the pork chops to the skillet and sear for about 3-4 minutes per side, or until golden brown and cooked through. The internal temperature should reach 145°F (63°C) for medium-rare or 160°F (71°C) for medium.
3. Add Sage Butter:
    - Reduce the heat to medium. Push the pork chops to one side of the skillet and add the butter to melt.
    - Once the butter is melted, add the sage leaves and minced garlic to the skillet. Cook for about 1 minute, stirring the sage leaves gently in the butter until fragrant and crispy.
4. Deglaze the Pan:
    - Pour in the chicken broth or white wine to deglaze the skillet, scraping up any browned bits from the bottom with a wooden spoon.
5. Make the Sauce (Optional):
    - Stir in the Dijon mustard and heavy cream (if using). Simmer for 2-3 minutes until the sauce thickens slightly. Taste and adjust seasoning with salt and pepper if needed.
6. Serve:
    - Remove the pork chops from the skillet and place them on serving plates.
    - Spoon the sage butter sauce over the pork chops.
    - Garnish with chopped fresh parsley.
7. Enjoy:
    - Serve the Pork Chops with Sage Butter hot, accompanied by your favorite sides such as mashed potatoes, roasted vegetables, or a crisp salad.

This Pork Chops with Sage Butter recipe is simple yet elegant, featuring tender pork chops with a flavorful sage-infused butter sauce. Perfect for a delightful dinner for two!

Seafood Risotto

Ingredients:

- 1 cup Arborio rice
- 4 cups seafood or chicken broth (warmed)
- 1/2 cup dry white wine
- 1 shallot, finely chopped
- 2 cloves garlic, minced
- 1 tablespoon olive oil
- 1 tablespoon unsalted butter
- 1/2 pound mixed seafood (such as shrimp, scallops, and/or mussels), cleaned and deveined
- Salt and pepper, to taste
- 1/4 cup grated Parmesan cheese, plus extra for serving
- Fresh parsley, chopped, for garnish
- Lemon wedges, for serving

Instructions:

1. Prepare the Seafood:
    - If using shrimp, scallops, or mussels, ensure they are cleaned and deveined. Season with salt and pepper.
2. Cook the Seafood (if applicable):
    - In a large skillet, heat olive oil over medium-high heat. Add the seafood (shrimp, scallops, or mussels) and cook until just opaque and cooked through, about 2-3 minutes per side. Remove from skillet and set aside.
3. Prepare the Risotto:
    - In a separate large, heavy-bottomed pot or Dutch oven, heat the olive oil and butter over medium heat.
    - Add the finely chopped shallot and minced garlic. Cook for 2-3 minutes until softened and translucent.
4. Toast the Rice:
    - Add the Arborio rice to the pot. Stir to coat the rice with the oil and butter mixture. Cook for 1-2 minutes until the rice grains become slightly translucent.
5. Deglaze with Wine:
    - Pour in the white wine and stir constantly until the wine is absorbed by the rice.
6. Add Broth (1 cup at a time):
    - Begin adding the warmed seafood or chicken broth to the rice, one cup at a time. Allow each addition to be absorbed before adding the next, stirring frequently. This process will take about 18-20 minutes in total, and the rice should be creamy but still slightly al dente when done.
7. Incorporate Seafood:

- When the risotto is almost done (about 15 minutes into cooking), stir in the cooked seafood (shrimp, scallops, and/or mussels). Continue to cook until the seafood is heated through.

8. Finish the Risotto:
    - Remove the pot from heat. Stir in the grated Parmesan cheese until melted and well combined. Season with salt and pepper to taste.
9. Serve:
    - Divide the seafood risotto between two serving plates.
    - Garnish with chopped fresh parsley and extra grated Parmesan cheese.
    - Serve hot, with lemon wedges on the side for squeezing over the risotto.
10. Enjoy:
    - Enjoy your delicious Seafood Risotto for Two as a comforting and flavorful main course, perfect for a special dinner at home!

This seafood risotto recipe combines the creamy texture of Arborio rice with the rich flavors of mixed seafood, creating a delightful dish that's sure to impress. Adjust the seafood selection based on your preferences and availability.

Spinach and Ricotta Stuffed Shells

Ingredients:

- 14-16 jumbo pasta shells
- 1 cup ricotta cheese
- 1 cup chopped spinach (fresh or frozen, thawed and squeezed dry)
- 1 cup shredded mozzarella cheese, divided
- 1/4 cup grated Parmesan cheese
- 1 egg, lightly beaten
- 1/2 teaspoon garlic powder
- 1/2 teaspoon dried basil
- 1/2 teaspoon dried oregano
- Salt and pepper, to taste
- 1 and 1/2 cups marinara sauce (homemade or store-bought)
- Fresh basil or parsley, chopped, for garnish

Instructions:

1. Prepare the Pasta Shells:
    - Cook the jumbo pasta shells according to package instructions until al dente. Drain and set aside to cool slightly.
2. Prepare the Filling:
    - In a mixing bowl, combine ricotta cheese, chopped spinach, 1/2 cup shredded mozzarella cheese, grated Parmesan cheese, beaten egg, garlic powder, dried basil, dried oregano, salt, and pepper. Mix until well combined.
3. Stuff the Shells:
    - Preheat your oven to 375°F (190°C).
    - Spread about 1 cup of marinara sauce evenly on the bottom of a baking dish.
    - Stuff each cooked pasta shell generously with the spinach and ricotta filling mixture.
4. Arrange in Baking Dish:
    - Place the stuffed shells in the prepared baking dish in a single layer.
5. Top with Sauce and Cheese:
    - Spoon the remaining marinara sauce over the stuffed shells, covering them evenly.
    - Sprinkle the remaining 1/2 cup shredded mozzarella cheese over the top.
6. Bake:
    - Cover the baking dish with aluminum foil and bake in the preheated oven for 25 minutes.
7. Final Bake:
    - Remove the foil and bake uncovered for an additional 10-15 minutes, or until the cheese is melted and bubbly.
8. Serve:
    - Remove from the oven and let it cool for a few minutes.

- Garnish with chopped fresh basil or parsley before serving.
9. Enjoy:
    - Serve the Spinach and Ricotta Stuffed Shells hot, with a side salad or garlic bread if desired.

This Spinach and Ricotta Stuffed Shells recipe is a comforting and satisfying meal for two, perfect for a cozy dinner at home.

www.ingramcontent.com/pod-product-compliance
Lightning Source LLC
LaVergne TN
LVHW061945070526
838199LV00060B/3983